Digital Professional Portfolios
for Change

Elizabeth Hartnell-Young
and
Maureen Morriss

Digital Professional Portfolios for Change

Published by SkyLight Professional Development
2626 S. Clearbrook Drive, Arlington Heights, IL 60005-5310
Phone 800-348-4474, 847-290-6600
Fax 847-290-6609
info@skylightedu.com
http://www.skylightedu.com

Senior Vice President, Product Development: Robin Fogarty
Director, Product Development: Ela Aktay
Senior Acquisitions Editor: Jean Ward
Project Coordinator: Sue Schumer
Editor: Jodi Keller
Cover Designer and Illustrator: David Stockman
Book Designer: Bruce Leckie
Formatter: Donna Ramirez
Proofreader: David Morrow
Indexer: Candice Cummins Sunseri
Production Supervisor: Bob Crump
Production Assistant: Christina Georgi

Printed in the United States of America.

ISBN 1-57517-165-1
LCCCN: 99-70997

2479-V
Item number 1753

Z Y X W V U T S R Q P O N M L K J I H G F E D C B A
06 05 04 03 02 01 00 99 15 14 13 12 11 10 9 8 7 6 5 4 3 2 1

Contents

Foreword

Over 25 years ago I went in search of my first job as an Industrial Arts teacher. I entered this field because I loved art, design, and technology. I took a portfolio along, and while most administrators did not know quite what to do with it, they all read it! This was a tremendous accomplishment in light of the fact that most résumés and college placement files only served as dusty paperweights at that time. Now, as we embark on a new century, the portfolio is marching out of the background and taking its rightful place in the foreground as a valued tool for hiring, employee evaluation, staff development, and personal growth.

My first portfolio was created using a typewriter, paste-up pages, and a bit of correction fluid. Today, you can encode your portfolio in the magic of HTML Internet language to create a far more powerful digital portfolio or multimedia document than was previously possible. In *Digital Professional Portfolios for Change,* Elizabeth Hartnell-Young and Maureen Morriss provide step-by-step technical instructions detailing how to turn the story of one's experiences in education into a persuasive digital document. In addition, they demonstrate how even advanced portfolios can be assembled using the everyday technology found in most schools. This portfolio can then be used in job interviews and performance evaluations, or as a guide in planning professional growth.

In addition to these uses, the authors illustrate how portfolios can be used to allow one to become "an active participant" in one's own self-assessment. Compared to a text-only document, the artifacts used in a digital professional portfolio provide the reader with greater insight into the achievements and successes of the portfolio developer. A multimedia portfolio project can contain multiple forms of evidence, including songs sung or composed by students, video clips showing student-peer critique sessions, duplicates of actual self-assessment rubrics used by students or staff, and charts or photos showing progress on a school-wide improvement program. These types of artifacts provide the reader with multiple evidence of the educator's skills and talents.

When I first started writing about portfolios, I suggested that they were far superior to the standard résumé and placement file. Yesterday's career documents are limited to text, but tomorrow's go-getters know they can best reach people when they use a mixture of media. This truth is profoundly demonstrated by the Internet itself. In the early days the "Net" was limited to text documents, and was used mostly used by non-profit organizations and researchers. But once it transformed itself from a text-based exchange into a web-based information resource, the popularity of the Internet exploded. People want a visual display of information, not page after page of uniform text. The portfolio clearly delivers for twenty-first century readers by crafting its message out of a combination of words, sounds, and images.

In addition, the sample-rich format is just what is needed in an employment world that has grown suspicious of résumés concocted out of inflated prose and exaggerated claims. The portfolio is a refreshing, authentic alternative. By using samples from everyday work, the portfolio is able to display proof of skills and credentials.

I enjoyed creating my first portfolio in the '70s and later my more sophisticated samples in the '90s. It was a wonderful way to sum up a career in education. I would lay the artifacts of my profession before me on a table, sip a favorite beverage, and then stir and sift through items. I was looking for a schema, a pattern, a thematic structure out of which I could communicate my passion for teaching and learning. As I handled different objects, I could see how the creative writing project linked with the drama program, or how the parent brochure connected with the community outreach samples. I found that assembling the samples in a portfolio was a very satisfying way to reflect upon my experiences and creatively communicate my career story to others. As the authors so eloquently point out, "a portfolio gives you a chance to personally celebrate and honor your contributions."

And yes, the authors are not just dreamers, they are realists as well. They both note that developing a portfolio can be personally challenging. But, they also point out that crafting a portfolio will result in enormous personal and professional growth. I urge you to try their suggestions to both advance your career and reacquaint yourself with the magic of your contributions.

—Martin Kimeldorf
Teacher and author of *Creating Portfolios for Success in School, Work and Life* and *Portfolio Power.*

Preface

Early in our careers as teachers, we were determined to "make a difference" in the lives of our students. Although we had not yet met, we followed similar paths on our journey of lifelong learning, always committed to sharing our learning with others. While teaching in Australia and the U.K., Elizabeth realized that she enjoyed working with and encouraging others to try new ideas. Meanwhile, Maureen was teaching elementary school in Victoria, Australia, which led her to explore literacy learning and teaching as a craft to be shared with others. Over time we both became leaders in our schools, modeling our love of learning for the whole community. However, it was not until we were both working in teacher education at RMIT University in Melbourne, Australia, that we met.

We soon realized that together we could create exciting and worthwhile projects for teachers in schools and universities, and for teachers in training. In 1997 we set out to explore the possibilities of multimedia or digital portfolios. It seemed that this idea might provide a way of linking the growing demand for portfolios with teachers' needs to learn more about the potential uses of technology. We were intrigued and challenged by the prospects of what might lie ahead. With a small team of teachers in elementary, secondary, and tertiary educational settings—named "women@thecuttingedge"—we developed a sample portfolio and stored it on CD-ROM. Our sense of achievement was great, and we knew then that given a realistic purpose, teachers do become highly motivated to learn more about technology and achieve great things using it, which can, in turn, encourage student learning.

Our team has gone on to develop a professional development program for other teachers. This book is the result of our collaboration so far. For us, it is another beginning as we realize there is so much more to learn. However, we feel confident that we can continue to make a difference in the lives of teachers and students. As Peter Senge says, "People with a high level of personal mastery are acutely aware of their ignorance, their incompetence, their growth areas. And they are deeply self-confident. Paradoxical? Only for those who do not see that the journey is the reward" (1994, p. 142).

Acknowledgments

It is important to acknowledge that much of our growth and the subsequent ideas presented in this book would not have been possible without constant feedback and support from a variety of people all around the world. In our quest for professional growth we have taken some risks that have demonstrated to us the potential of collaborative professional development to create personal and organizational change. We always work to enable others to reach their dreams and aspirations, just as the following people have encouraged us with this project. Our thanks go to: Jean Ward and Kay Burke from Skylight Professional Development who reached out across the ocean to Australia and encouraged us to share our ideas with a wider audience; Helen Smith and our colleagues at RMIT (Royal Melbourne Institute of Technology) University, Melbourne, Australia; Alan Cattell from Bradford University in the U.K. who provided us with a network to correspond with and learn from; and Jodi Keller who communicated with us by e-mail and courier to provide excellent service as our editor.

Most importantly, we would like to acknowledge the original team members of women@thecuttingedge who began this journey with us and gave us a forum where we could test our ideas and approach.

Elizabeth Hartnell-Young and Maureen Morriss
Melbourne, Australia

Introduction

This book is designed for administrators, teachers, educators, graduates, or students with a passion for learning as well as for teaching. Those working in support roles, such as teacher assistants and administrative staff, can also benefit from it. This book provides readers with the framework and tools needed to develop a digital portfolio that records professional growth and development goals and celebrates achievements.

Even those with little computer experience and limited equipment can use multimedia technology to create a vibrant, individualized, high-quality portfolio that can be continually and easily updated. Throughout the portfolio development process, portfolio developers will gain greater knowledge of themselves and their learning processes while expanding technology skills. Portfolio development can assist anyone preparing for performance review, looking for a job, or seeking a promotion. It also can help organizations aid their staff in focusing on development goals.

While this book shows how to construct a portfolio, it takes the portfolio approach further than the typical presentation folder. Portfolios are linked with one of the urgencies of the Digital Age: the need for administrators, superintendents, teachers, and students to better understand the possibilities of learning technologies. The portfolio development process, as explained in this book, can help developers feel more confident with their technological skills, thus making them more open to sharing their skills with others.

Portfolio development has become an important means of increasing organizational learning and effectiveness. All those responsible for professional development in education, whether in schools, school districts, or universities, will find the contents of this book valuable as they plan for professional and organizational growth in the Digital Age.

What This Book Is About

Across the world, people are being asked to take responsibility for their own professional growth, understand more about themselves and their achievements, and take steps to develop new knowledge and skills. Teachers and administrators have found that producing a portfolio helps to clarify their values, enhances their capacity to reflect on their learning, increases their self-knowledge and self-esteem, and gives them added confidence in their work with colleagues and students. Authors such as Bridges (1995) believe that changes in the nature of employment mean that soon everyone will need a portfolio that demonstrates their skills, achievements, and particularly their versatility to achieve employment.

In his book *The Empty Raincoat,* Charles Handy (1994) says that intelligence has replaced land as the source of wealth. Knowledge workers—educated professionals and managers—own the new property. They can sell it, trade it, or give it away, and fortunately, still possess it. The Digital Age is a time of information revolution where the constraints of time and space have been demolished by transport and the Internet. People in the U.S., Canada, the U.K., and Australia can learn of the same new ideas at the same time and engage in meaningful conversations with others about these ideas around the globe.

In this context teachers are in an awesome position. They have a great deal of knowledge and the skills to share this knowledge. Schools are centers of learning, and whole communities benefit from this learning. However, this can only occur if teachers understand their capabilities. Teachers in schools and universities, principals and superintendents, and support staff in educational institutions are being called on to demonstrate their knowledge. Each individual brings a different combination of knowledge, skills, and experiences to their work. But it is not enough just to collect knowledge. Knowledge must be *used* in order to make a difference.

This book won't turn the reader into a multimedia designer. However, it will show educators how to use multimedia (or digital technology) to describe their unique experiences and to reflect on how they grow and develop in their professional life. Portfolio development challenges developers to consider the impact of their work—how they make a difference. Finally, this book helps teachers understand ways in which technology might assist them to record and communicate their professional achievements, and how they can share what they have learned with students to help them unlock the secrets of multimedia.

Chapter 1

Professional Portfolios and Today's Technology

Teacher development—a process of self-understanding grounded in the teacher's life and work.
—Hargreaves and Fullan 1996, p. 3

For many years, teachers and other professionals have had opportunities for professional development in the form of conferences and courses. The focus of this development was often on curriculum innovations and specific classroom methods and practices that met the immediate perceived needs of teachers. Recently, the focus has been on longer-term learning, such as individual growth in self-understanding, setting goals for professional development, planning learning activities and projects, and reflecting on outcomes.

In a national survey in the United States (Rényi 1996), teachers were asked what they valued in professional development and what they thought would be most effective in improving their ability to serve students. Respondents used phrases like "keeping up" to define professional growth: keeping up with technology, with the latest trends, and with their particular fields. The terms "updating," "continuing," "becoming," and "improving" were used frequently. Teachers reported that a wide range of activities assisted in their professional growth, such as formal courses, seminars, workshops, and degree programs. However, they also recognized the enormous potential for learning in their day-to-day work.

By examining and reflecting on this work, teachers can learn much about their strengths and skills, and also about areas in which they can grow and learn. Such self-knowledge is an important tool that can be used to further professional development.

Teaching in the Digital Age

In the Digital Age, valuing individual capabilities and talents is becoming more important than ever. Ways of organizing work are changing, making permanent employment less common and creating a sense of opportunity for some and great insecurity for others. Individuals are becoming increasingly responsible for managing their own career path. According to Bridges (1995), the organization is no longer a structure built out of jobs, but a field of work that needs to be done. Teachers are being asked to be self-sufficient and entrepreneurial and to engage in ongoing learning to keep up with change. The expectations of teachers' roles are changing for those preparing to be teachers, the institutions that train them, and the schools and communities that employ them.

Technology is also contributing to the changing expectations of teaching and learning. Technology has created wonderful opportunities for learning, but access to a range of media is available to relatively few. Many academics and teachers are working with students who are more familiar with technology than they are. With the recent knowledge explosion, a teacher in the twenty-first century cannot possibly have all the information that students clamor for. Many who have been teaching for over twenty years are faced with the challenge of being learners at a time in their career when they hoped to be experts in their work.

As new skills and knowledge are required for curriculum development and assessment, new pedagogies are being created as teachers and students use technology for research and learning. The problem of data overload is real, and teachers are forced to make difficult choices about the use of technology, which can be used to support inquiry, link learners in many settings, and record and assess progress. Which of these should be emphasized? Trying out new things, reflecting on activities, and making sense of the successes and failures is essential to the teacher's role of incorporating new technology into the classroom. Exploring this methodology and the learning that results is important as teachers seek to develop useful resources for the future.

However, there are some practical barriers to professional growth in the Digital Age. Teachers are knowledge workers: educated professionals with knowledge and expertise, dealing with the creation and communication of information. Often teachers are so busy working for others that they do not deeply reflect on or articulate clearly what they know. Additionally, teachers are constantly challenged to use new technology in their work, but they cannot find time to learn or funding for resources. To overcome these barriers, it is essential for teachers and students to work together on their learning.

The concept of lifelong learning includes participation in new activities as well as taking part in reflective practice. Teachers who engage in reflective practice spend time considering what they value as teachers and how this influences their approach to teaching, learning, their career paths, and their aspirations. Reflective practice includes recording thoughts, goals, successes, and failures. This allows teachers to understand more about themselves as learners and to communicate this to others. Some teachers engage in reflective practice by writing regularly in a journal, others document critical incidents and their responses, while others collect snippets of information that are important to them in some way, such as quotes, photographs, or letters from students. For example, Figure 1.1 is a journal entry that Sylvia, a newly appointed principal, made shortly after the announcement of her promotion. Sylvia noted in her journal that the school's head custodian was surprised to find out that she was the person he had seen visiting the school one weekend. Perhaps Sylvia's gender, her casual clothing on the weekend, or her general manner were not features he equated with his schema of 'principal.' For Sylvia, the custodian's comment was a reminder that she might not fit everyone's image of a principal, so she noted it in her journal.

FIGURE 1.1

Extract from a Principal's Journal

> First day:
> Ted said, "I saw you up here one Saturday, but I didn't think you were the new principal."

Noting such moments, however small they may appear, can be important in focusing reflection on professional growth. As these moments are revisited over time, they reveal layers of development. What appeared difficult, or surprising at first, can seem trivial, or perhaps more serious, after several months have passed. Notes in a journal can help identify signs and increase the teacher's ability to deal with particular situations. Through reflection teachers can also review the outcome of their work and the impact they have had on the lives of others. In doing so, they are contributing to their profession and bolstering their self-esteem.

Focusing attention on the self is not as selfish as it may seem, for as Covey (1992) expresses it, "...until we take how we see ourselves—and how we see others—into account, we will be unable to understand how others see and feel about themselves and their world" (p. 58).

As teachers become more involved in planning, recording, and reflecting on their own learning, portfolios have become popular as a means of keeping and presenting information about professional growth (Wolf 1994; Burke 1996; Kimeldorf 1995). Green and Smyser (1996) see the teaching portfolio as a tool for staff development, based on the premise that the best knowledge is self-knowledge, and believe that teaching portfolios empower teachers to change by encouraging reflective thinking.

The notion of portfolios can be taken even further in relation to technology. There are numerous questions about the use of technology in learning: How can telecommunications be used to support learning? How should this be managed? How might the curriculum need to change? Currently professional development is still more likely to be *about* learning technologies than achieved *through* the technologies, and this should be reversed. Following Hargreaves and Fullan (1996), this book suggests that models of professional development which involve learning about technology by using technology to work on real projects are likely to be more successful than those which focus on skill-building without any real sense of the teacher's context. Technology often drives the learners, rather than acting as their servant. This results in courses in Excel, Word, or Internet Usage, rather than purposeful courses in keeping budget records, writing reports, or researching funding sources—courses in which such software programs can be used. The challenge is to find vehicles that motivate teachers to learn, vehicles that relate to a teacher's life and work.

Producing a digital portfolio links the need for professional development with the need for increased skills and enhanced understanding of technology. This type of portfolio not only provides teachers with a vehicle to shape their goals, but also helps them to further their goals by aiding them in becoming technologically savvy.

Purposes for Portfolios

Portfolios are commonly used by artists to showcase work and are now becoming more popular in schools, universities, and the professional world as a way to record achievements, plan professional development, and engage in reflective practice. While a portfolio is normally a collection of evidence of achievements, it is much more than a résumé.

A portfolio can include statements of vision and values which describe and explain beliefs about education, why various activities are included, reflections on the outcomes of the activities, and what was learned from them. The "evidence" can include curriculum materials or reports, photographs of students at work, feedback from colleagues or employers, and even videotapes of presentations.

Many professionals present their portfolios in plastic binders, which are carefully constructed to display their strengths in a range of areas. These types of portfolios can be easily rearranged and added to, but they can be difficult to reproduce and to transport. Using technology provides teachers with many more options for recording and presenting artifacts that demonstrate their achievements and growth. For this reason, students and teachers are increasingly encouraged to develop and submit electronic or digital portfolios for assessment (Niguidula 1993; Barrett 1998).

Many people discover that one of the most important and long-lasting outcomes of producing a portfolio is the self-esteem that comes from recording and reflecting on achievements and career successes. Experienced teachers and administrators are finding that the benefits of developing a portfolio include the opportunity for professional renewal through mapping new goals and planning for future growth.

While there are many reasons to develop a portfolio, the most important are developmental—as a means for teachers to plan their own growth. Many teachers and administrators are working in systems where personal accountability outside the classroom is becoming more controlled, and portfolios are being thought of by education administrators as a means of presenting information for teacher assessment. When teachers perceive that accountability is viewed as more important than their knowledge and expertise, they can become cynical, and their portfolios tend to be heavy with documentation but light on passion. When teachers feel valued and rewarded, and then accountable, they feel more positive about their work. Therefore, this book focuses on the learning and development opportunities available to teachers, individually and in groups, through creating portfolios.

The following reasons for portfolio development have been suggested by an experienced teacher and are a useful starting point for those who wish to learn more about the benefits of portfolio development.

- Portfolios empower teachers by encouraging reflective practice: the very act of constructing a portfolio is a great process of self-discovery as the teacher makes critical decisions as to what to include.
- Portfolios encourage teachers to capitalize on their strengths.
- Portfolios allow teachers to self-identify areas for improvement and encourage professional growth.
- Portfolios integrate all aspects of teaching: they provide a way to look at the whole teacher.
- Portfolios accommodate diversity.
- Portfolios allow teachers to become active participants in their own assessment.
- Portfolios model a method of assessment and reflection that teachers may be asking of their students.
- Portfolios present a new approach to evaluating teachers.
- Portfolios can be used in addition to a résumé and as an interview tool (Wells, personal communication, July 30, 1998).

Perhaps one of the most important purposes for a portfolio is for personal celebration and appreciation of the contributions made throughout one's career, as this teacher found:

> "My portfolio binder was prepared for me to take into an interview. During three interviews no one asked to see it, even though I had it with me and told them I had it. At first I was disappointed that no one had

taken the time to look at it. Then I realized that building my portfolio had been a professional growth experience that had made me focus on all my areas of strength as a teacher" (Wells, personal communication, July 30, 1998).

The multiple purposes for which portfolios currently are used are summarized in Figure 1.2, below.

FIGURE 1.2

Purposes for Portfolios

Formative (developmental) Purposes	***Summative (assessment) Purposes***	***Marketing Purposes***
1. Professional Development Planning	4. University Admission	8. Job Application
2. Recording Continuing Professional Development	5. Meeting Course Requirements	9. "Cold Calling"
3. Celebration of Achievements	6. Performance Review and Promotion	10. Organizational Capability
	7. Professional Certification and Registration	

These purposes cover ten areas. They are the following:

1. Professional development planning

Many teachers undertake self-assessment activities as they set professional development goals and conduct research related to their teaching. The portfolio enables them to define their professional development needs.

2. Recording continuing professional development

The portfolio can be used to record the steps in the process of professional development, as well as reflections that teachers engage in along the way. The recording of all professional development activities, with an indication of time spent and learning outcomes achieved, is often suggested or required by school and professional associations.

3. Celebration of achievements

Many teachers find that keeping a record of highlights of their work in a portfolio, with captions and reflections, is a wonderful boost to their self-esteem.

4. University admission

For many years, students in the visual arts have been expected to present a portfolio of design, photography, or artwork in addition to their entrance interview. More and more high school graduates in various disciplines are providing portfolios in addition to their examination scores to provide evidence of their capabilities.

5. Meeting course requirements

Many university courses require a portfolio that provides evidence of coursework and contains accompanying reflections to be submitted to meet assessment requirements.

6. Performance review and promotion

In many schools and universities, the presentation of a portfolio that provides evidence of meeting the criteria or standards is often required of staff in a regular review meeting. It is also often a requisite when an application is submitted for promotion.

7. Professional certification and registration

Some human resources, management, education, and health-related professional organizations have devised a portfolio framework for their members, in which they must provide evidence of achievement for membership, for continuing registration, or to upgrade their membership to a higher status.

8. Job application

Often applicants for a position prepare a portfolio providing evidence of skills, competence, and personal development. They take this to an interview, or even sometimes send it with the application. A good portfolio can make writing a résumé a simpler task.

9. "Cold calling"

Portfolios demonstrating skills and achievements have been used in the visual arts as part of the introduction process between client and artist. Entrepreneurial educators can use portfolios in a similar fashion to display their abilities when "cold calling": meeting a prospective client for the first time.

10. Organizational capability

Organizations can make important use of the portfolio. They can use it to readily view the skills of their staff, as well as to market the capability of the school or organization to parents and the community.

The importance of ascertaining a purpose is also expressed by David Baume who writes the following:

> "Preparing a portfolio should always involve acts of judgement, periods of critical reflection, or processing experience and learning from experience. It can be a moving experience—a long look into the mirror, with the

image enhanced for greater clarity (sometimes welcome, sometimes not). But if the sole or primary purpose of preparing the portfolio is for assessment, then the portfolio will take one form. If the purpose is to plan for one's professional development, or to prepare and make a case for promotion, or to generate a growing journal of practice from which to learn, then the different forms may be appropriate. I am just a little nervous of a portfolio prepared without purpose, and of the neighboring concept that one universal portfolio can serve a variety of purposes. This may be true of a dead collection of materials; it can surely never be true of a portfolio whose selection and shape and form and critical and linking commentaries and explanations were all prepared for a particular purpose" (Baume 1997).

Whatever the purpose, what is exciting and challenging is the capability to record, store, and present the portfolio in a multimedia form. In order to do this, it is important that a wide range of evidence of work and accomplishments are gathered. This evidence can be organized into files by categories. This creates a Personal Archive from which material can be taken to create a purposeful portfolio. A well-organized Personal Archive lays firm foundations for portfolio development and use. From this a digital portfolio can be developed which meets the needs of both the developer and the intended audience. The figure below (1.3) demonstrates how artifacts can be drawn from the Personal Archive to produce a range of portfolios for different purposes.

FIGURE 1.3

Developing a Personal Archive

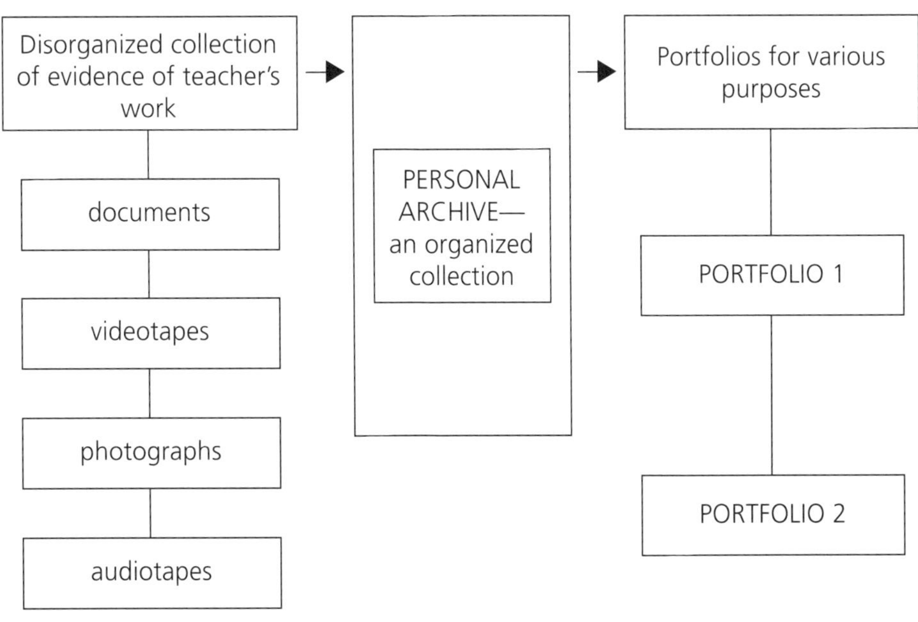

Multiple Intelligences and the Multimedia Portfolio

Multimedia is a general term that covers the combination of text, graphics, sound, and video in digital form, such as on a CD-ROM or via the Internet. Multimedia can be a powerful aid in integrating the various areas of a teacher's work, as it enables links to be made between different items. The result of teachers producing multimedia portfolios is greater understanding of the potential of technology.

Creating a multimedia portfolio enhances professional growth by linking the need for increased technology skills with the need to develop a portfolio for a particular purpose. An added advantage of the multimedia portfolio is that the evidence can be presented to an audience in a multifaceted format, using text, photographs, sound, and video. This type of presentation capitalizes on Howard Gardner's (1984) work on Multiple Intelligences (see Figure 1.4) in that the material presented caters to multiple ways of sharing and understanding the vision, values, and achievements of the teacher or administrator. For example, the textual aspect of a multimedia portfolio may appeal to a learner's verbal/linguistic intelligence because of the need to express growth and development via reflective comments. Another learner with a predisposition for visual/spatial learning may find that the digital images and non-linear visual aspects of the graphics and video components suits his style. In this way, different aspects of the multimedia portfolio appeal to different learners. Figure 1.4, on the following page, demonstrates which aspects of multimedia cater to which intelligences.

Now that multimedia is a part of education and society, teachers are challenged to explore the ways in which it can enhance learning. Beverley Johnson, principal of Emmaus College in Sydney, Australia, has based the introduction to computers in her school on the research on multiple intelligences and brain-based learning. She believes computers can help learning by making information more accessible, increasing students' motivation, and allowing them to publish their work in ways that result in greater self-esteem (Armitage 1998). Handy (1994) argues that we should start from the assumption that everyone is intelligent in at least one area, and it should be the first duty of any school to discover and develop this intelligence in each of its students. Multimedia resources can assist teachers as they work to create learning experiences that meet the needs of all students. Meeting this challenge requires a positive attitude towards all students, a valuing of diversity, and in many cases, a search to identify the student's strengths and talents. It follows that if teachers are to recognize and value the intelligences of their students, they will benefit from doing the same for themselves.

How Multimedia Can Cater to Gardner's Multiple Intelligences Theory

Intelligence	*Description*	*Multimedia Contribution*
Logical/Mathematical (scientific thinking)	This intelligence deals with inductive and deductive thinking and reasoning, numbers, and the recognition of abstract patterns.	• Text and data • Tables and graphs • Comparative analysis of teacher's work over time • Links to related documents
Verbal/Linguistic	This intelligence is related to words and language, written and spoken.	• Text, both written and oral • Creative forms of expression • Sound • Variety of text forms, formats, fonts, and design
Visual/Spatial	This intelligence relies on the sense of sight and being able to visualize an object.	• Graphics • Links within the portfolio and to other sites • Logos, images • Creative forms of expression
Bodily/Kinesthetic	This intelligence is related to physical movement and the knowings/wisdom of the body.	• Producer is "learning by doing" • Ability to move through the portfolio (not a static page) • Reader can create own movement through portfolio
Musical/Rhythmic	This intelligence is based on the recognition of tonal patterns, sounds, and a sensitivity to rhythm and beats.	• Sound which captures mood, style, feelings, etc. • Video
Interpersonal	This intelligence operates primarily through person-to-person relationships and communication.	• Photographs of self • Photographs of others involved • Comments about self and feedback from others
Intrapersonal	This intelligence relates to inner states of being, self-reflection, metacognition, and awareness of meta-spiritual realities.	• Reflection by self and others • Planning and production requires metacognition • Integration of values and action through linked material
Naturalist	This intelligence relates to recognizing relationships and systems within one's environment.	• Organization of materials and links into a system of levels of information

FIGURE 1.4

Another result of creating a multimedia portfolio is that teachers gain skills that assist them in understanding more about using the Internet for online learning and how to develop appropriate curriculum materials and learning situations. Those who take on the challenge to create a multimedia portfolio will need to spend some time considering their own work, which results in a greater understanding of reflective practice and portfolio development which can be shared with both their colleagues and their students.

An Australian secondary teacher recently completed his multimedia portfolio, and it is clear that the purpose and the skills acquisition demonstrated in the portfolio are complementary to his professional growth. He explains:

> "I made the decision to go ahead and develop my portfolio, not so much as a means of presenting information for future promotion, but more as a means of gathering together information about my teaching life. So, it was more of a self-esteem development measure, to just reassure myself that I was in fact a good teacher and that I had made, and could still make, a strong contribution not only to the school I was teaching in, but to any school.
>
> Over a period of many years I have set myself a project to do each year, which I can look back on at the end of the year and say to myself 'if nothing else, I have at least achieved this task.' In 1998 I set myself the task of developing an electronic professional portfolio. This would also give me a task on which I could base some professional development in technology. I believe that I learn the use of technology better when I have a concrete task to do rather than doing some undirected training with nothing to follow it up" (C. Davies, personal communication, December 12, 1998).

The skills required to develop a multimedia portfolio need to be demystified. The necessary skills are not complex, and the computer equipment in many schools and organizations is well able to cope with producing a multimedia portfolio, as can be seen in Chapter 2. One place to begin to develop these skills is through research on the Internet.

Researching Portfolio Development on the Internet

The Internet is a useful place to find examples of portfolios for education and other fields. Use a search engine (a tool on the Internet like a library catalog) and type in keywords such as "teaching portfolio," "professional portfolio," and "career portfolio," as well as other related keywords. (Each search engine has its own way of refining searches to avoid turning up millions of examples. Check the on-screen instructions to improve the quality of the search.) A search for these terms will turn up many examples of portfolios, as can be seen in Figure 1.5. Various search engines can be used, such as Yahoo™, Lycos™, Excite™, Altavista™, and Hotbot™. The examples shown in Figure 1.5 were found by entering the keywords "professional portfolio" as a search on Altavista™. For those who are not familiar with Internet searching, it might be wise to ask a student or colleague to assist; the basic skills can be practiced in under an hour.

FIGURE 1.5

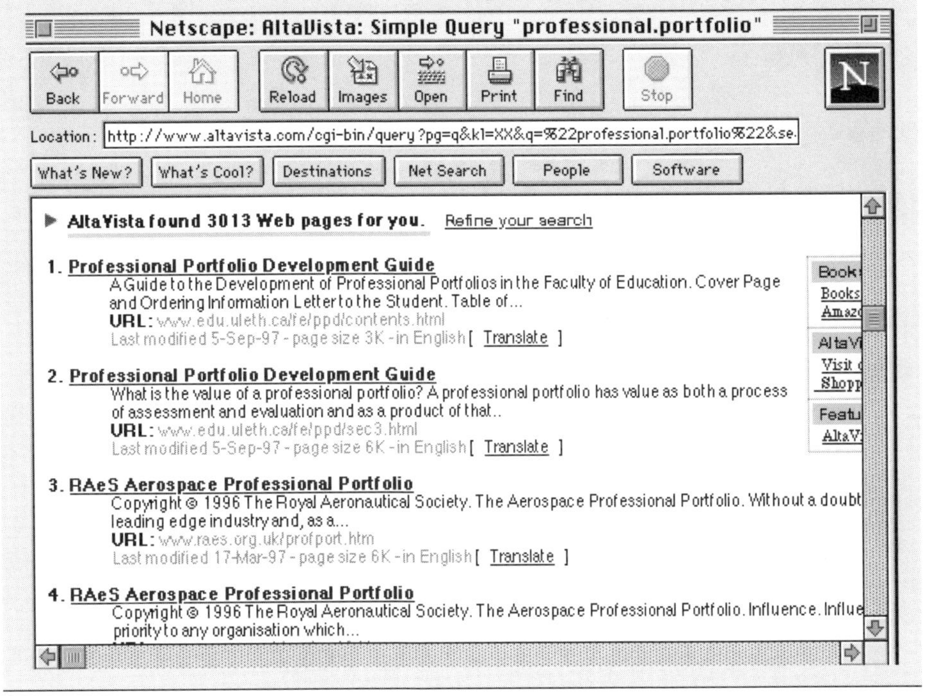

A search of the Internet as described above will also locate articles and advice about creating portfolios. Broadening the search by using keywords such as "technology" and "professional development" will lead to further information, supporting more professional growth and understanding.

While a portfolio can be developed alone, experience indicates that greater learning occurs when groups of people work together. The Internet is beneficial in this way because it allows for communication between widely-dispersed portfolio developers, allowing individuals to ask questions, share ideas, and provide feedback. This book advocates that anyone—teacher or student—can benefit from preparing a portfolio in conjunction with other learners.

Chapter 2

Why Use Multimedia?

Q: What type of training activities are most helpful for teachers who are learning about technology?
A: Three types: Hands on, hands on, and hands on.

In this era of demand for computer-literate teachers, the multimedia portfolio provides powerful evidence that the teacher is confident with technology. Most importantly, students benefit from having teachers and administrators who are familiar with learning technologies and are able to use them appropriately in the curriculum. Creating a digital portfolio provides individuals with a reason to learn more about the technology that surrounds us. This book provides a step-by-step outline of basic portfolio production techniques that do not require high-tech equipment: in fact, most of the necessary tools can be found in many schools today.

Teachers and Digital Technology

The imperative to use technology in the classroom has caused many teachers concern. Many teachers grew up without using computers in school. What they know about computers has been learned since, often in an incoherent manner. Therefore, the computer skills of many teachers are often less developed than those of their students. Many agree that professional development in technology lags behind the need for skills and knowledge (Armitage 1998).

Some teachers are afraid their lack of technological knowledge will be exposed in front of their students, and they respond to this situation by discouraging student access to computers in the classroom. Meanwhile, students with computers at home continue to develop their technology skills, while those without such access remain "computer illiterate." Whatever the teacher's attitude toward computers, this type of situation must not be allowed to continue in our knowledge society.

Thus, in order to learn themselves and to aid their students in learning, teachers are plunged into the role of learners. For some, this is an unnatural balance of power; for others, it is completely congruent with their view of life-long learning. Knowledge of adult learning indicates that if the purpose of the learning is clear and it meets the needs of the learner, the learning is more likely to be successful. Hargreaves and Fullan (1996) have shown concern that much professional development is imposed via a top-down model, which assumes that knowledge transfer occurs as a direct result of instruction by experts, with little recognition of the existing skills of the learner. This model shows disrespect for teachers' professionalism, learning styles, and actual needs. At times, professional development is imposed by administrators driven by budget considerations who are anxious to achieve enormous change in a short time. This approach is often characterized by a discourse of certainty in which the trainer directs the learners through a set sequence of skills and knowledge, using terminology that confuses rather than clarifies. As a result, the learner feels inadequate. These views of professional development must be challenged. The focus needs to be placed on increasing the current skills and knowledge of the learner and working towards clearly identified purposes, which are the key elements in the process of professional development.

Extensive research, such as that reported in *Teachers Take Charge of Their Learning* (Rényi 1996), has found that high-quality professional development is that which

- has the goal of improving student learning at the heart of every school endeavor;
- helps teachers and other school staff meet the future needs of students who learn in different ways and who come from diverse cultural, linguistic, and socioeconomic backgrounds;
- provides adequate time for inquiry, reflection, and mentoring and is an important part of the normal working day of all public school educators;
- is rigorous, sustained, and adequate to the long-term change of practice;

- is directed toward teachers' intellectual development and leadership;
- fosters a deepening of subject-matter knowledge, a greater understanding of learning, and a greater appreciation of students' needs;
- is designed and directed by teachers, incorporates the best principles of adult learning, and involves shared decisions designed to improve the school;
- balances individual priorities with school and district needs and advances the profession as a whole;
- makes the best use of new technologies;
- is site based and supportive of a clearly articulated vision for students.

With these principles in mind, one way to introduce technology is to place the teacher at the center of the activity; to produce something that will be useful to the teacher, and will enhance her self-esteem. The multimedia résumé or a professional portfolio provides such an opportunity. Some enthusiasts claim that all résumés will soon be on the Internet, and in some schools, teachers are being asked to prepare their own web pages with a current résumé as a way of practicing their technology skills. Putting a résumé or portfolio on the Internet is one way to show achievements, and if the technical work is done by the owner of the portfolio, it is a great way to develop skills and knowledge.

Examples of Multimedia Portfolios

A multimedia portfolio is a thoughtful collection of artifacts designed to meet a particular purpose. The difference between this type of portfolio and others is that it can display material professionally by combining a range of media. Media can include text documents, photographs and other images, and sound or video recordings, as shown in Figure 2.1 on the following page.

Figure 2.2 on the following page (Maddern 1997) shows a page from a multimedia portfolio containing a photo of the teacher's class at work, an introduction and description of the artifacts provided, and an image of the cover of a curriculum publication she produced. From this page, she created links (not shown) to an activity in the publication and to other related examples of her work.

FIGURE 2.1

Hypertext enables the material in this portfolio to be linked to create a pathway through related artifacts. Hypertext is the system often seen on the Internet as colored and underlined words that can be selected to reveal further layers of information. This system enables large amounts of information to be presented through links, rather than as a linear document. See Chapter 6 for more information on producing Hypertext (HTML) documents for a portfolio.

FIGURE 2.2

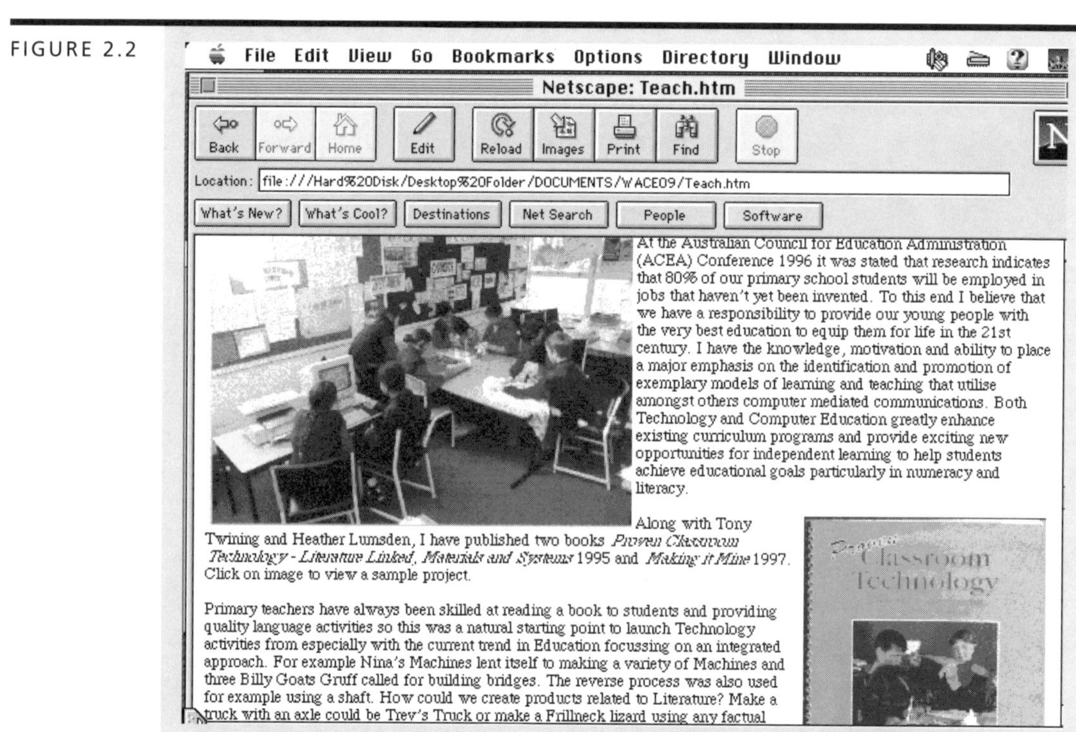

Figure 2.3 is a page from another teacher's portfolio (Taylor 1997) displaying some student work which illustrates her commitment to encouraging students to try new ways of presenting their assessment tasks. She has reproduced part of an assignment that includes a link to a sound file. When the link to this file is engaged, a few seconds of music is played.

FIGURE 2.3

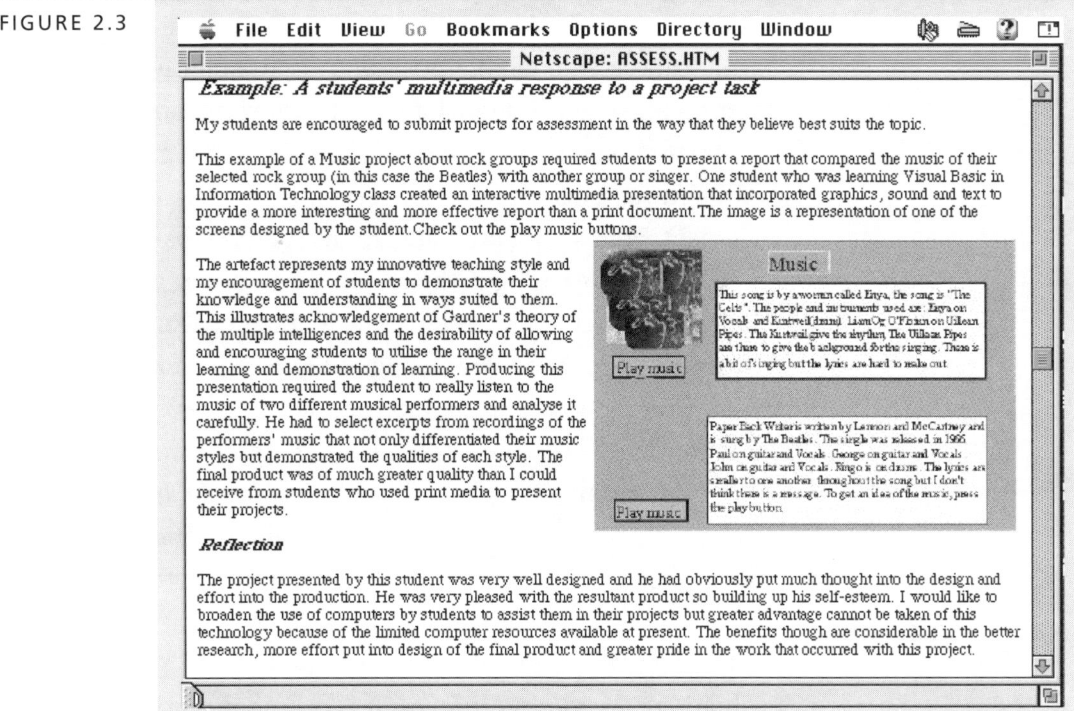

File Edit View Go Bookmarks Options Directory Window

Netscape: ASSESS.HTM

Example: A students' multimedia response to a project task

My students are encouraged to submit projects for assessment in the way that they believe best suits the topic.

This example of a Music project about rock groups required students to present a report that compared the music of their selected rock group (in this case the Beatles) with another group or singer. One student who was learning Visual Basic in Information Technology class created an interactive multimedia presentation that incorporated graphics, sound and text to provide a more interesting and more effective report than a print document. The image is a representation of one of the screens designed by the student. Check out the play music buttons.

The artefact represents my innovative teaching style and my encouragement of students to demonstrate their knowledge and understanding in ways suited to them. This illustrates acknowledgement of Gardner's theory of the multiple intelligences and the desirability of allowing and encouraging students to utilise the range in their learning and demonstration of learning. Producing this presentation required the student to really listen to the music of two different musical performers and analyse it carefully. He had to select excerpts from recordings of the performers' music that not only differentiated their music styles but demonstrated the qualities of each style. The final product was of much greater quality than I could receive from students who used print media to present their projects.

Music

This song is by a woman called Enya, the song is "The Celts". The people and instruments used are: Enya on Vocals and Kintwell(drum) Liam Og O'Flynn on Uillean Pipes. The Kintwell give the rhythm, The Uillean Pipes are there to give the background for the singing. There is a bit of singing but the lyrics are hard to make out.

Play music

Paper Back Writer is written by Lennon and McCartney and is sung by The Beatles. The single was released in 1966. Paul on guitar and Vocals. George on guitar and Vocals John on guitar and Vocals. Ringo is on drums. The lyrics are similar to one another throughout the song but I don't think there is a message. To get an idea of the music, press the play button.

Play music

Reflection

The project presented by this student was very well designed and he had obviously put much thought into the design and effort into the production. He was very pleased with the resultant product so building up his self-esteem. I would like to broaden the use of computers by students to assist them in their projects but greater advantage cannot be taken of this technology because of the limited computer resources available at present. The benefits though are considerable in the better research, more effort put into design of the final product and greater pride in the work that occurred with this project.

Although a multimedia portfolio can contain many forms of information, the entire portfolio can be stored in a variety of ways—on computer disks, Jaz™ or Zip™ disks, on a laptop computer, or on a CD-ROM. All of these methods take up much less space than a paper-based portfolio. Chapter 5 has more information on ways to store digital portfolios.

Benefits of Digital Portfolios

Educators have the opportunity to create interesting and varied multimedia portfolios for many purposes as they record and reflect on their daily work. Hypertext allows for deeper understanding and explanation through links that go from summary statements to complete documents, related items, and reflections. In addition to displaying artifacts efficiently, links can allow the collection of material in a Personal Archive to become broader and more thoughtful. Developing a multimedia portfolio can be challenging, requiring teachers to model learning, develop technology skills along with their students, and share the results with a wider audience.

Some audiences are not yet familiar with Internet, laptop, or CD-ROM portfolios, and this must be taken into account. However, the use of these technologies is increasing rapidly, so the innovative teacher can showcase achievements and share ideas all over the world. In Australia, applicants for educational leadership positions are frequently being asked to prepare a presentation to the selection panel, and some are taking the opportunity to prepare a simple multimedia portfolio explaining their vision, values, and achievements using a PowerPoint™ program or a hypertext linked document. This is then presented to the selection panel via laptop computer.

As student learning is the raison d'être of a teacher's work, the speedy application of what the teacher has learned is also an important benefit of multimedia portfolios. Producing a digital portfolio enables the teacher to understand more about the Internet and its uses, the capacity of common computer hardware, the uses of common software applications, and some of the potential of multimedia. This leads to increased application of appropriate technology in the classroom through preparing materials, researching new information, and presenting it to students in a range of formats.

Understanding more about multimedia also assists in developing and evaluating classroom resources. It is even appropriate to have students actively involved in the recording and collection of artifacts on some occasions, and to share with them the reasons for the collection. For example, students can videotape the teacher engaged in classroom activities, devise assignments that observe and reflect upon their learning processes, and collect data that monitors classroom interactions. Feedback from students and colleagues should be valued and considered. Modeling recording and reflection to students demonstrates the importance of these activities, and this can encourage a dialogue with students about learning processes.

School administrators find that encouraging teachers to produce portfolios not only encompasses the benefits mentioned above, but also can lead to a greater understanding of the skills and talents of the teachers and the intellectual capital in the organization. Some schools encourage teams to produce portfolios around particular projects, while others develop multimedia marketing packages to promote the school curriculum, personnel, and facilities.

The benefits of developing multimedia portfolios are summarized in Figure 2.4 on the following page.

FIGURE 2.4

Benefits of Developing Multimedia Portfolios

Benefits from the educator's point of view	*Benefits from the organization's point of view*
• ability to present a wide variety of forms of evidence, linked for easy access • evidence addresses a range of audience intelligences • evidence can be shown to be authentic • increases skills and knowledge of multimedia production and its use • enhances the image of the teacher as an innovator, and as being confident with technology • the teacher can be more "employable" • students and teachers work together on meaningful activity	• increases confidence of teachers in implementing technology • students see a positive role model when teachers work with technology in this way • enhances the "learning organization": students and teachers learn together when all create portfolios • increases knowledge of the "intellectual capital" • the product can be used in marketing the capabilities of the organization

While multimedia portfolio production can be undertaken by teachers working alone, portfolio projects are also ideal for teams. Multimedia portfolio projects can benefit from the diversity of skills of team members as they act as coaches and mentors for each other. The outcomes include enhanced technology skills, understanding new ways of teaching and learning, and professional portfolios that effectively capture the knowledge and capabilities of the teachers who produce them. Chapter 3 explains how to get started on portfolio production.

Chapter 3

Integrating Your Personal Vision into Your Portfolio

First we may ask, who are we, and what are our gifts? What are our distinctive competencies; what do we have to contribute that is unique or different? What special knowledge do we have? What do we value? What do we believe in?—Harrison 1984, p. 107

Educators around the world realize that tomorrow's workplaces and communities need citizens who can increase their knowledge from many different perspectives, who can continue to learn in a rapidly changing environment, and who can think critically and strategically to solve problems. Citizens of the twenty-first century must be prepared to collaborate locally and around the globe, and the implications of this for teaching and learning are a constant topic of discussion. What should teaching and learning be like in the Digital Age? What knowledge is important? What is the role of technology in learning? How are schools preparing their students for a global future? These are some of the fundamental questions teachers and administrators are considering as they face the future. This chapter focuses on ways to articulate vision, understand self, and track responses to these questions as a means of demonstrating professional growth. Records of this information and reflection on it are necessary and should be stored in a Personal Archive. This archive, a professional history, will help educators better understand themselves and their roles to help them make positive contributions to the future.

Focusing Your Vision

For educators, the future is as important as the present. Why, otherwise, would they expend so much energy on understanding the needs of their students and preparing learning activities to extend their skills and knowledge? School administrators are expected to develop a shared vision with staff, students, and parents which guides and links the community. For cohesion to be effectively achieved, the individual must be able to clarify and articulate a personal vision. As Fullan (1995) states,

> "Shared vision is important in the long run, but for it to be effective you have to have something to share. It is not a good idea to borrow someone else's vision. Working on vision means examining and reexamining, and making explicit to ourselves why we came into teaching. Asking 'What difference am I trying to make personally?' is a good place to start" (p. 13).

The teacher who embarks on portfolio development to plan and record professional growth is modeling a way of integrating vision, values, purpose, and action. Senge's (1994) use of the term "personal mastery" describes the attitude of such a teacher.

> " 'Personal mastery' is the phrase my colleagues and I use for the discipline of personal growth and learning. People with high levels of personal mastery are continually expanding their ability to create the results in life they truly seek. From their quest for continual learning comes the spirit of the learning organization" (p. 141).

Additionally, learning to develop a multimedia portfolio enables teachers to take risks with technology and to better understand its demands as well as its rewards. By capturing the experience of the learning journey, reflecting on its meaning over time, and sharing the learning with others, teachers will develop new insights and understanding. Access to technology is enabling individuals and groups to implement change in both the philosophy and practice of teaching. Technology should support rather than drive the curriculum, the learning environment, and professional development. A teacher's multimedia portfolio is not expected to be a graphic designer's dream: the emphasis should be on learning.

One of the challenges educators face is articulating a personal vision and a way of constructing and reconstructing the purposes of their work, both individually and collectively. Writing an educational vision statement is a valuable activity for all teachers. It forces them to clarify what they are working toward and to articulate goals that can be shared and debated with colleagues. As teachers engage in portfolio development, they consider the congruence of their vision and actions.

An individual's educational vision statement will change as goals are achieved and new targets are set. Therefore, it's a good idea for teachers to write a vision statement that targets future goals while taking into account the context of the current time and place. The vision is directed towards the future, but it must be undertaken in the present. In other words, the teacher must act on the vision from the moment it is conceived. An updated vision statement should be regularly placed in the Personal Archive (the starting point for any portfolio). The Personal Archive is the place where vision-directed learning is captured, and this can be shared in a portfolio.

Using Self-Knowledge to Define Your Portfolio

Personal mastery begins with knowing and understanding oneself. For educators, knowledge of values and knowledge of learning styles are two important aspects of self-knowledge.

Values are the ideals that give significance to our lives, which are reflected through the priorities we choose, and that we act on consistently and repeatedly. Two key aspects of portfolio development are the articulation of vision and values, which allows purposes and ambitions to be made clear, and the idea that the portfolio is the means of communicating these to others. The exercise in Figure 3.1 (following page) is just a sample of the many tools that can help educators clarify the values that drive their life and work. Each value requires a simple choice: is this value of high or low importance to me? The answers to these questions will allow individuals to shape a portfolio that reflects their values.

For those seeking professional growth, consideration of learning style is another important aspect of self-knowledge. Honey and Mumford (1986) devised a questionnaire designed to identify learning styles, of which they believe there are four distinct preferences. The four styles are termed Activist, Reflector, Theorist, and Pragmatist. Although all four are required for the complete learning process, Honey and Mumford suggest that when an individual's preferences are catered to, they will learn more successfully. Recognizing predominant learning styles can help teachers find appropriate professional development activities to meet their learning needs. The areas of lower preference provide opportunities for further development. For example, a teacher who is naturally an activist learner would benefit from the practice of reflection. While the four styles represent four inherent aspects of the learning process, many people have a dominant learning style that they feel most comfortable with. These four learning styles are briefly described in Figure 3.2 on page 31.

Values Clarification Activity

Value	*Definition*	*Importance (High or Low)*
Achievement	Feelings of personal or professional accomplishment	
Advancement	Opportunity to move up or on	
Affection	Giving and receiving warm feelings	
Authority	Being seen as a person with power	
Balance	Giving time to various parts of life	
Challenge	Enjoying the demands of personal and professional life	
Change	Enjoying and adapting to different situations	
Competition	Engaging in activities which test my abilities against others	
Conformity	Fitting in with others	
Cooperation	Working in a friendly/compatible environment	
Creativity	Opportunity to be innovative	
Entrepreneurship	Coming up with new ideas and projects	
Expertise	Feeling on top of a discipline or area of responsibility	
Health	Taking care of physical and mental health	
Helping others	Feeling that others benefit from the work done	
Independence	Having freedom to do things	
Influence	Getting others to agree	
Image	Looking impressive	
Leadership	Articulating a vision and encouraging others to share it	
Knowledge	Opportunity for ongoing learning	
Recognition	Constructive feedback on successes and failures	
Risk-taking	Opportunity to try things out	
Support	Being backed up in decisions and actions	
Teamwork	Sharing goals, responsibilities, and outcomes with others	
Working alone	Taking individual responsibility	

FIGURE 3.1

Honey and Mumford's Learning Styles

ACTIVIST
These people learn best when:

- there are new experiences, problems, or opportunities from which to learn
- they can become engrossed in short "here and now" activities such as competitive teamwork tasks, role-playing exercises
- there is excitement, crisis, and variety
- they have high visibility, e.g., chairing meetings, leading discussions, giving presentations
- they are allowed to generate ideas without constraints of policy or structure or feasibility
- they are thrown in at the deep end with a task they think is difficult
- they are involved with other people, e.g., bouncing ideas, solving problems as part of a team
- it is appropriate to "have a go"

REFLECTOR
These people learn best when:

- they are allowed or encouraged to watch/think/chew over activities
- they are able to stand back from events and listen or observe
- they are allowed to think before acting or commenting, e.g., a chance to read in advance
- they can carry out some painstaking research
- they have the opportunity to review what has happened
- they are asked to produce carefully considered analyses and reports
- they are helped to exchange views with other people within a structured learning experience
- they can reach a decision in their own time without pressure and tight deadlines

THEORIST
These people learn best when:

- what is being offered is part of a system, model, concept, or theory
- they have time to methodically explore the associations and interrelationships between ideas, events, and situations
- they have the chance to question and probe the basic methodology, assumptions, or logic behind something
- they are intellectually stretching, e.g., by analyzing a complex situation, being tested in a tutorial session
- they are in structured situations with a clear purpose
- they can listen to or read about ideas or concepts that emphasize rationality or logic and are well-argued
- they can analyze and then generalize the reasons for success or failure
- they are offered interesting ideas and concepts even though they are not immediately relevant
- they are required to understand and participate in complex situations

PRAGMATIST
These people learn best when:

- there is an obvious link between the subject matter and a problem or opportunity on the job
- they are shown techniques for doing things with obvious practical advantages
- they have the chance to try out and practice techniques with coaching/feedback
- they are exposed to a model they can emulate, e.g., a respected leader, a demonstration from someone with a proven track record, lots of examples/anecdotes, or a film showing how it is done
- they are given techniques currently applicable to their own jobs
- they are given immediate opportunities to implement what they have learned
- they can concentrate on practical issues, e.g., drawing up action plans with an obvious end product, suggesting short cuts, giving tips

FIGURE 3.2 (Honey and Mumford 1986)

It is clear that there are many links between understanding diversity, individual differences, multiple intelligences, and the range of learning styles. Tools such as those found in this chapter are always beneficial to raise the awareness of individuals to help them better understand both themselves and their multiple audiences. A portfolio demonstrating professional growth describes both how individuals work and teach, and how professional development or work activities have been planned to increase their learning.

Additionally, the portfolio can be designed to communicate with people with different learning styles and needs. For this reason it is very important to maintain a Personal Archive containing a range of materials in a variety of forms. In undertaking this aspect of planning and presentation, the educator steps into the shoes of the audience, and by observation and reflection, develops further understanding of others. These are important outcomes of portfolio development.

Gathering Material for a Personal Archive

The Personal Archive is the starting point from which material for various types of portfolios can be drawn. There are numerous lists of materials that can be referenced when building up a collection of evidence for the Personal Archive (Kimeldorf 1995; Burke 1996; Brown and Irby 1997; Campbell et al., 1997). They generally include artifacts such as those outlined in Figure 3.3, on the following page.

As material is collected and stored, it is important that sufficient detail about the item, including both the scope and the impact of the activity, is recorded for future use. For example: Is the date clear? How many students were involved? How many staff members? What role was played by the teacher? What were the outcomes in the short term? In the long term? Teachers are engaged in activities at many levels: classroom, teaching teams, school-wide, local community, state, national, and international. Figure 3.3 provides a framework to make sure that the artifacts reflect this range, particularly as teachers move toward leadership roles.

In order to create a portfolio that can meet multiple purposes, it is important to collect evidence of activities and achievements as they occur. In some cases, however, teachers have not kept records or have moved from one school to another, leaving important evidence behind. If this is the case, reflective writing can help to keep the experience alive. While there might not be a specific artifact to represent an activity or event, reflections on what was intended, what was learned, and how it relates to the present

Possible Items in a Personal Archive

Author	*Self*	*Students*	*Parents, Teachers, Community*
Personal characteristics and values	• vision statement dated • values exercise dated • self-assessments • goal statements • professional development plan • résumé • reflection	• letters • testimonials • cards • gifts	• references • letters • awards • certificates
Classroom activities	• curriculum materials • lesson plans • case writing and notes of observations • photographs and videotape of activities and products • reflective writing	• examples of student work • tests • student self-evaluations and learning logs • evaluations and feedback of teacher • photographs of bulletin boards	• newspaper reports • television footage • thank you letters
School-wide policy and programs	• policy documents • committee reports and records showing roles and responsibilities • press releases • reflective journal	• opinion surveys • articles in newsletters • photographs of extra-curricular activities	• opinion surveys • statistics
Contribution to the profession and wider community	• articles in professional journals and books • presentations to colleagues and peers • memberships		• awards

FIGURE 3.3

are valuable and can be included in the archives. Fortunately, many schools also have archives. School archives may contain photo albums and press clippings of important school activities in recent years. These archives can be used to obtain the evidence required to build up one's own Personal Archive. (See Figure 3.4 on the next page.)

FIGURE 3.4

If material from the past is not available, begin recording for a Personal Archive in the present. There needs to be some focus or structure to this activity, or it will get out of hand very quickly. Some teachers use a portable file to store paper evidence, while others use plastic binders, boxes, or filing cabinets. These are all very bulky means of storage, so it is useful to set aside time to organize artifacts and to convert papers to digital format, as described by a teacher below.

> "Initially I gathered any information (artifacts) that I could, consisting of letters, certificates, class materials. Most of the recent material I had in electronic form. The older material I have scanned onto a disk and it is now stored electronically. This will be an on-going process as I find new or alternative materials that I can use. Once I had a reasonable amount of material I began to classify it into categories: Developing Others, Personal Professional Development, Teaching and Learning, etc. That process has worked pretty well" (C. Davies, personal communication, December 12, 1998).

Without good organization, the amount of evidence in an archive can quickly become unwieldy. Some educators arrange material chronologically, others by project, and others according to standards and competencies. The system of organization is a personal decision, but it is important that information can be retrieved quickly.

The collected material will be in a variety of forms. In addition to text, audio- and videotapes can capture teachers in action. Storing and presenting all these materials can become quite cumbersome. Storing short selections in digitized form on computer disk is one solution to this problem. This creates a catalog of artifacts of text, sound, photos, or video as a series of files. Some simple methods of storing graphic and sound material efficiently are described in Chapter 5.

Reflecting on Your Portfolio

Various forms of reflection are necessary to produce a complete portfolio. When developing a portfolio, it is necessary to reflect on individual artifacts and their contribution to the portfolio's purpose. Reflective writing can itself be an artifact within the portfolio that demonstrates growth and development. Finally, it is important to reflect on what the complete portfolio portrays. The examples below demonstrate these different types of reflection.

Reflection on Individual Artifacts

Reflection on artifacts can be based on a framework of questions such as these:

- Why did I choose this evidence?
- What was I trying to achieve with this activity?
- How does this fit with my education values?
- How well did I achieve my goals?
- What were the critical factors helping or hindering achievement?
- What have I learned/what would I do differently next time?
- What are the implications of what I have learned for me, my job, and the teaching profession?

The artifact that teacher Kelly Mandia bases her reflection on (below) is an essay-writing lesson plan. From it, she highlights her students' ability to communicate and express their knowledge:

> "My training and experience have shown me that students learn best when they are active participants in what they are learning. My emphasis is on the development of skills (learning and communication), critical thinking, and self-esteem using the social studies curriculum. I have worked with my students to improve essay writing skills (*click here to view the essay-writing lesson plan*), which is imperative to communication and the expression of knowledge" (Mandia 1998).

As demonstrated by this example, reflecting on each artifact before it goes into the portfolio will help to ensure a cohesive and well-organized completed portfolio.

Reflective Journal as Artifact

Reflection is much more than a few sentences on the results of an activity. A thoughtful reflection is like a dialogue with the self that creates links between the past, present, and future, and between theory and practice, vision, values, and action. Reflection should enrich the archive by adding material about the scope and impact of events and activities, showing how they made a difference.

The following selection clearly demonstrates a reflection from one educator's journal, used as an artifact for her teaching portfolio.

> "When organizing my teaching portfolio, I recognized the need to place 'critical reflection' at the forefront. For example, my professional journals have been the life blood of my teaching from the time when I first entered the profession. From one of the pages of my journal I wrote about the most rewarding aspects of teaching:
>
> I am learning that it is often beneficial to be controversial in order to get students to stop believing 'on faith' what is taught. I am aware of the great power I wield as a teacher and feel the need to stir and unsettle their sensibilities; to leave them anxious for a time without a safety net. When this is accomplished, it allows students to face their beliefs squarely and come to some kind of resolution." (G. Latham, personal communication, June 1, 1998).

When reflective journals are used as artifacts in a portfolio, they serve to further develop and explain teachers' professional goals and the steps and activities they have engaged in to achieve these goals.

Reflection on the Portfolio

When reflecting on a complete portfolio, the focus should be on its purpose, the values and vision it represents, the professional growth it outlines, and the rubrics against which it might be evaluated. A concluding reflection can also be added to the portfolio, which sums up the developer's feelings about professional development through the portfolio. The following example is a concluding reflection to a principal's portfolio in which she provides evidence of her professional growth and leadership:

> "We have made many changes, both to curriculum, to the way we do things and to the manner in which we work together. Staff has experi-

> enced a 'mindset' change. They now understand why we must walk our talk, why quality is important all the time without question, why lifelong learning is honored through professional development opportunities, why we must share our learning if we are to be a true learning community, and why we look upon everything through our 'systems' eyes. We are not just a part of something, we are a 'whole'. People now understand the complexities of the decisions we make, how one small change affects many other areas of our lives. Now people look for the many different points of view, the many results that we will have due to the changes we make. Our staff now see things in 'big picture' mode. What a wonderful experience! And what a challenge this was" (McLean 1998, p. 6).

This type of reflection can help the audience to understand what the teacher has learned from the development process, and how she plans to implement what she has learned in her work.

There are many ways to collect information for the Personal Archive. However, for those who want to take advantage of technology to record information for the Personal Archive, there are a number of possibilities. They include creating an electronic journal using a palm-held or laptop computer, creating an audio journal using a small audio recorder, keeping a camera or video camera on hand to record classroom highlights, and encouraging students to become involved in electronic data collection. The riches of such an archive, along with reflection on the portfolio and the artifacts in it, will assist in the development of a quality portfolio.

After reflecting on goals and values and creating a Personal Archive, teachers will be ready to begin organizing information for the development process. Chapter 4 contains information on steps that can be followed to ensure the development of a focused and complete portfolio.

Chapter 4

Ten Steps to Producing a Multimedia Portfolio

People often wonder who I really am, and why I have so much energy and passion for the job I do.
—McLean 1998, p. 1

Once the portfolio developer has finished gathering a wide range of artifacts for the Personal Archive, he will be able to produce portfolios for many different purposes. This chapter describes ten steps that are necessary to prepare a high quality professional portfolio suitable for multimedia presentation format. Many of the steps also apply to the more traditional print-based portfolios. (See Figure 4.1, next page, for a summary of the ten steps.)

The portfolio development process provides a framework for planning and action. The steps that follow are based on the experiences of practicing educators in schools and universities. They found that producing a portfolio helped to clarify their values, enhanced their capacity to reflect on their learning, increased their knowledge and self-esteem, and gave them added confidence in working with colleagues and students. They also found that producing a portfolio takes time. But, as Kenneth Wolf states, "although portfolios can be time consuming to construct and cumbersome to review, they can also capture the complexities of professional practice in ways that no other approach can" (Wolf 1996a, p. 41).

Ten Steps to Developing a Professional Portfolio

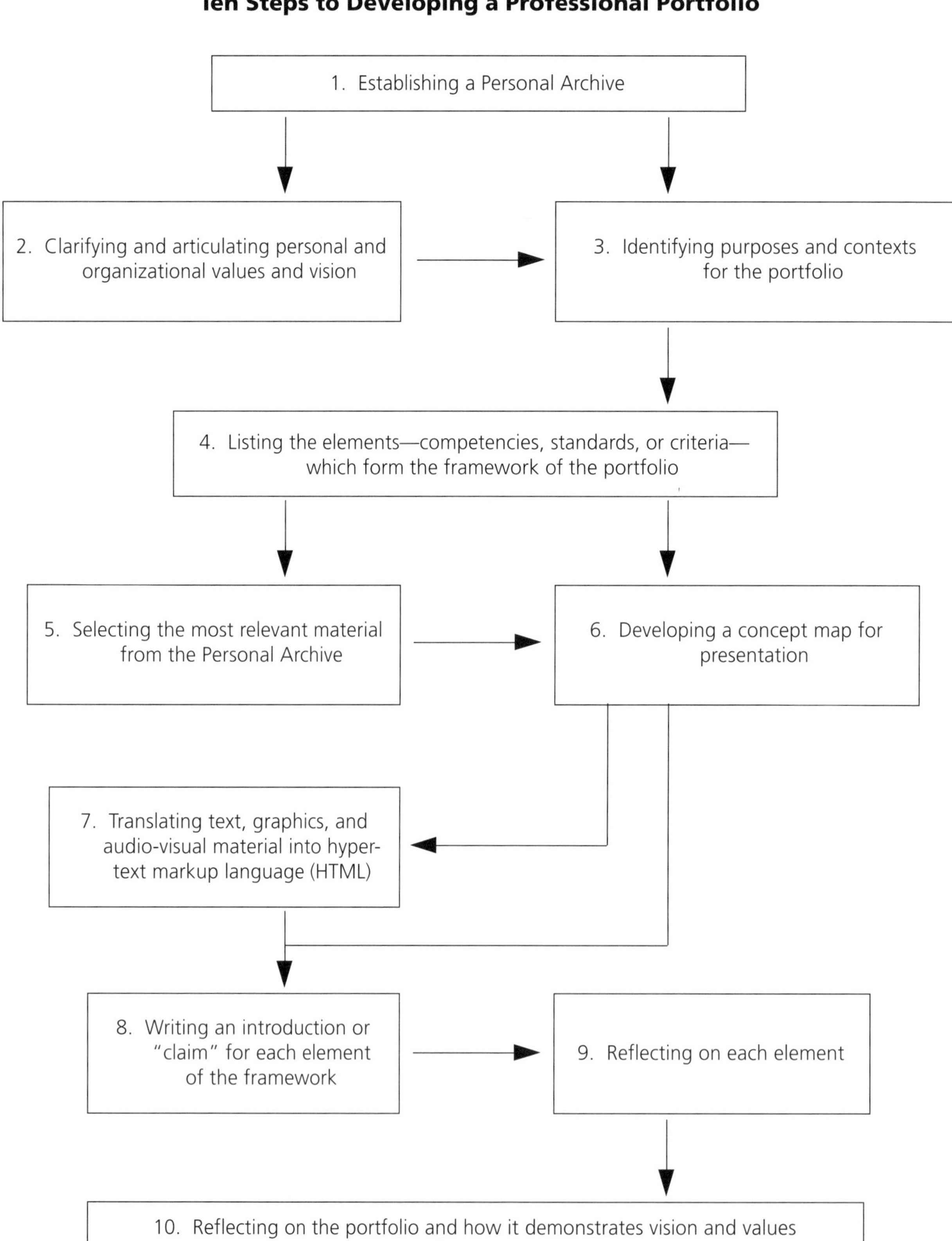

FIGURE 4.1

At the most basic level, three types of content are important in any portfolio:

- An introduction outlining purpose, values, and philosophy
- Artifacts displaying evidence consistent with the purpose, values, and philosophy
- Reflection on the evidence and on the learning and development

It is important to remember that developing a portfolio is a process that is personally challenging and, as a result, can lead to enormous personal growth. Therefore, in the activity surrounding collecting material and producing a quality presentation, it is important to always keep in mind the individual the portfolio is representing. Preparing a professional portfolio is an ongoing process that involves collecting artifacts and evidence of accomplishments and reflecting on these. The journey or process of putting together the portfolio is just as important as the end product. The ten steps outlined below describe this process in more detail.

1. Establishing a Personal Archive

It is essential to have collected a Personal Archive before beginning development of the professional portfolio. In Chapter 3 we described the basis for establishing a Personal Archive, which includes documentation of values and vision, records of development and achievement, and reflective writing. A well-organized Personal Archive lays the groundwork for organized portfolio development and use. While developing the Personal Archive can be time-consuming, the investment is worthwhile. A good collection leads to many choices for portfolio development.

2. Clarifying and Articulating Values and Vision

Peter Senge says, quite simply, "vision…is the picture of the future we seek to create" (Senge 1994, p. 223). Today, both individuals and schools are encouraged to articulate their picture of the future as an inspiration and motivation for action. Similarly, values and philosophy have been renewed as important underpinnings of the work of individuals and organizations.

An expression of personal beliefs about education, a statement of values underlying one's work, or a vision statement is an excellent way to introduce and focus a portfolio. Sometimes teachers become so caught up in their daily work that they fail to articulate why they are working so hard.

Chapter 3 discussed ways in which developing a portfolio can help teachers think about how and why they are making a difference and what drives them towards their vision. The artifacts selected for the portfolio should show how the vision is being realized.

In the following extract, a principal describes her vision and values in the introduction to her portfolio:

> "I am a teacher. I am an educator. I am a leader. People often wonder who I really am, and why I have so much energy and passion for the job I do. I need to tell them that I have a passion for living, for life itself. I consider myself fortunate that I was able to find my niche in education. Most people do not truly believe that I do this because I love children and that I firmly believe that they deserve the very best life has to offer.
>
> My vision is that through education, we can have all children leading successful lives.
>
> My mission is simple—I need to make it happen" (McLean 1998, p. 2).

A vision statement, combined with a statement of purpose, provides the reader with a clear framework for understanding and reviewing the portfolio.

3. Identifying Purposes and Contexts

As noted in Chapter 1, portfolios are used to support professional development in many ways. There is also a growing movement towards using the portfolio to make judgements, such as in a performance review or for hiring purposes. However, the formative type of portfolio, which records development planning, risks taken, successes, and failures may not be appropriate for review or selection processes, which require a summative assessment. Teachers who have enthusiastically undertaken portfolio development often report that they need a different portfolio for each purpose. Fortunately, a well-organized Personal Archive makes this possible without too much difficulty.

A clearly understood purpose is essential in developing an effective portfolio, and guidelines are often provided to suit the purpose. For example, at The University of Bradford in England, clerical and administrative staff are assisted in developing portfolios that record and reflect on their professional development. Teams of people work together to identify issues and set goals, collaborate on projects, and reflect on the outcomes, both for themselves and for their organization. Members of the team are given a document with helpful advice, including this introduction:

> "The Portfolio is your personal property and as such is intended to help you in reflecting upon where you are now and where you would like to be, albeit in an environment which is challenging, complex and less predictable. The way in which you use the Portfolio is up to you. No one is going to check if you have completed it. However, it is worth asking yourself the question 'how many of us create the time to reflect upon ourselves and our aspirations?' All too many of us are driven by the task-completion nature of our jobs and the changes which are going on around us. Completing the Portfolio over a period of time is a worthwhile activity in that it is intended to help you stock-take your current skills and competence and identify areas of development which may be important to your future" (University of Bradford 1998, p. 1).

Some portfolios will be specifically designed to communicate with an audience. In this case it is essential to consider the interests, expectations, and experiences of those reading the material. Will a document in a presentation folder be the most suitable format? Is a video better? Would a multimedia presentation display achievements in a way that would be interesting and impressive?

It is important to consider how familiar the intended audience is with the material being presented and whether people from other parts of the world would be able to understand what is being portrayed. These considerations will influence the choice and style of language, abbreviations, and terminology. Some terms may have to be explained—even within the same country—to ensure that the desired meaning is conveyed.

4. Listing the Elements That Form the Framework

Once the purpose and context are clear, the structure of the portfolio can be planned. For a purpose such as an annual performance review, or an application for a specific position, the portfolio can be organized according to the competencies or key skills required. These types of portfolios are often very structured. Portfolios sometimes begin with a self-assessment of personal qualities, skills, and knowledge, using generic or specific elements, as a basis for personal planning. The development of Teacher Standards in many states has provided a structure for self-assessment and preparation for professional development, which underpins the portfolio development process. These structural criteria, competencies, and standards are called "elements" of the portfolio framework.

In the examples that follow, the educators each have a different purpose for their portfolios and, therefore, uses specific elements. In some cases, the elements are predetermined, and in others the person developing the portfolio needs to decide which elements to include.

Maria—Portfolio to Be Used for Performance Review

Maria is an experienced principal. She is preparing a portfolio based on the specific result areas (SRAs) and performance targets she agreed on for the current year with her superintendent (manager). At that time she was able to select from these SRAs:

- Educational leadership
- School image
- Educational management
- Staff management
- Business management
- Environment management
- Relationship management
- School improvement initiatives
- Special projects

After careful consideration of the school plan and district priorities and discussion with the leadership team, Maria chose to focus on:

- Educational leadership
- School image
- Business management
- School improvement initiatives

Therefore, the evidence she presents in her portfolio for presentation to her superintendent will need to display outcomes and achievements related to these areas.

Jack—Portfolio to Be Used to Provide Evidence of Meeting Professional Standards

Jack is an experienced classroom teacher. The Teacher Standards in his state fall into the following categories:

- Content knowledge
- Human development and learning
- Diverse learners
- Communication

- Learning environment
- Planning for instruction
- Instructional strategies
- Assessment
- Reflection and professional growth
- Professional relationships
- Technology
- Professional conduct

Jack is developing his portfolio for review with his principal, aiming to show his competence in all of these areas. Therefore, he is using the Teacher Standards as a basis for collecting material and planning his portfolio.

Lee—Portfolio to Provide Evidence of Professional Development Outcomes

Lee's portfolio is not mandated by her employer. She wants to use the portfolio as a focus for her professional development. After consideration of her personal goals, she decides that her portfolio for this year will be based on three elements that reflect her current priorities. These are:

- Learning technologies
- Assessment and reporting
- Links with parents

Lee will focus on these three elements when selecting artifacts for inclusion in her portfolio, and she plans to present the portfolio in an electronic form to show her commitment to learning more about technology. Maria, Jack, and Lee have clearly identified the elements that will form the framework for each of their portfolios and will follow this framework during portfolio development.

Early identification and recording of competencies, standards, or criteria is recommended. The selection decisions made when identifying such elements need to clearly reflect the audience, the context, and the purpose of the portfolio. The initial list of elements forms the framework for the portfolio, whether print-based or electronic. While many of these elements begin as seemingly static lists, they are developed and brought to life through the selection of artifacts that demonstrate growth and achievement.

5. Selecting Evidence from the Personal Archive

Once you have decided on the purpose and the elements of the portfolio framework, it is often necessary to make a selection from the items of evidence in the Personal Archive. Quality, not quantity, is the key. Important considerations include:

Evidence That Is Recent

Depending on the purpose, there might be guidelines within the organization about how far back in time it is reasonable to go for evidence. Unless the portfolio is designed to show a complete career history, recent evidence is preferable. While the letter of thanks from 1986 is a valuable part of the archive, it is unlikely to make it into the current portfolio.

Range of Evidence

A well-rounded portfolio will contain artifacts that show action and reflection, curriculum and administrative tasks, work with staff, students, and parents, and individual and team achievements. A selection of text, graphics, sound, and video evidence makes the portfolio interesting, as well as displaying different skills. Evidence of classroom, whole school, and large-scale activities should be chosen, as outlined in Figure 3.3 in Chapter 3.

Evidence Showing Impact

It is particularly helpful to provide evidence of the impact of a teacher's work in the portfolio. This shows that the activities undertaken in an attempt to achieve the vision have had an effect on the classroom, the school, or a broader audience. This can be shown through survey results, comparative statistics, or through feedback from others.

What to Include

In deciding whether to include an artifact, Brown and Irby (1995) suggest asking the question, "What does this piece of evidence add to my portfolio?" When the answer is "nothing," there is no need to include the artifact. When reviewing artifacts for inclusion, the focus should be on which artifacts from the Personal Archive best exemplify the elements of the framework, the values, and the vision of the portfolio developer.

The collection of artifacts is a substantial part of the process, but however well organized they are within selected elements, artifacts do not make a portfolio. Further planning is necessary to develop a complete portfolio.

6. Developing a Concept Map

Developing a concept map or graphically organizing the evidence assists in the presentation process. It is here that links and connections between artifacts and elements are highlighted and made specific. The reasons for such links need to be identified and expressed simply for the intended audience. A concept map or a storyboard provides a frame of reference for comprehending the portfolio, whether it is in a digital or print form. Figure 4.2 shows how the links might be planned:

FIGURE 4.2

Organizing the Portfolio Evidence

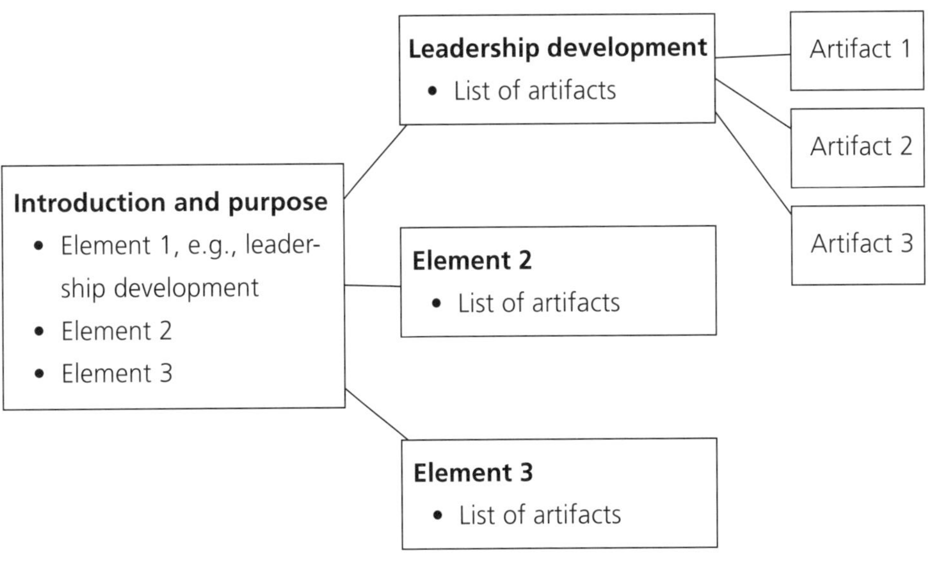

This is not at all complete, but it does show how the material can be arranged, linked, and then reviewed. Any gaps in the material selected or an imbalance between elements should become clear at this point. This step can provide direction for future professional development or suggest types of evidence that need to be collected for the Personal Archive. In Step 7 we see how such a concept map or storyboard is prepared for a digital or multimedia portfolio suitable for presentation on the Internet or CD-ROM. This step does not apply to print-based portfolios.

7. Translating into Hypertext Markup Language (HTML)

Hypertext markup language (HTML) is a language for describing structured documents suitable for the Internet. It can also be used to create links in multimedia documents saved on CD-ROM. HTML allows the reader to experience the links between the parts of a portfolio. Further information about using HTML is provided in Chapter 6. The example in Figure 4.3 below, shown on an Internet browser, was originally part of a document created in Microsoft Word™. It was copied and pasted into Netscape Composer™, along with several other related files supporting each claim. Links were made between the underlined words and their related files, as described more fully in Chapter 6. A simple click on the underlined word opens up the related information. In this way, the reader can follow areas of interest in any sequence.

FIGURE 4.3

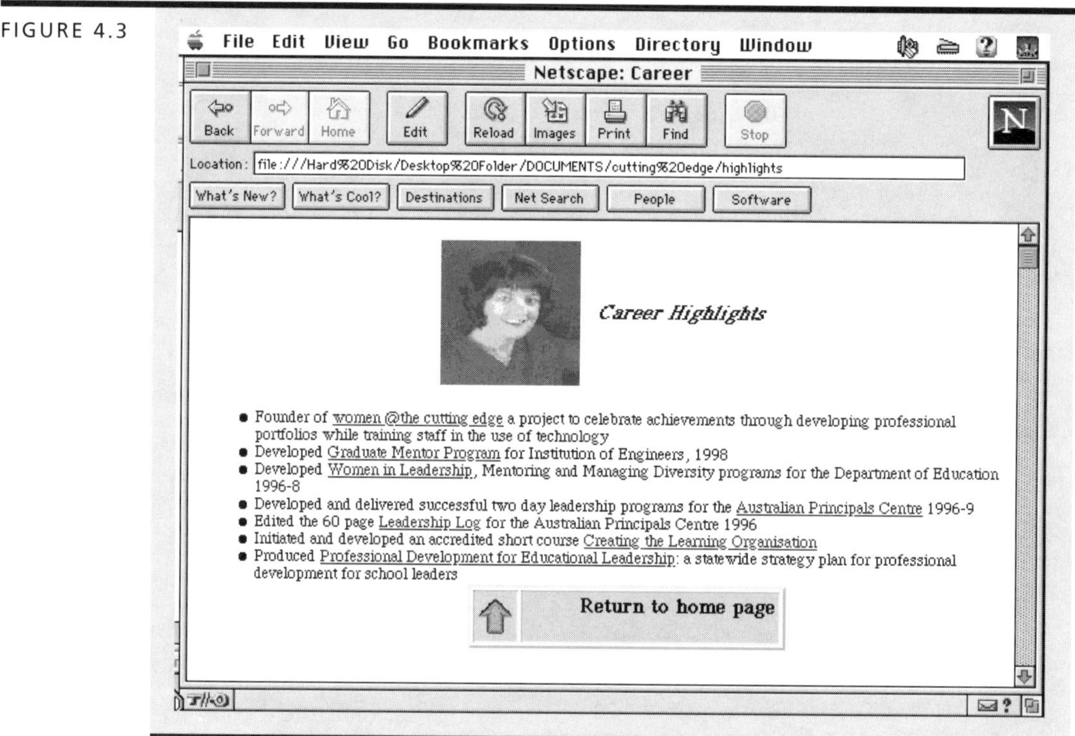

Figure 4.4 (on the next page) shows exactly the same information as Figure 4.3, but Figure 4.4 is in its HTML format and shows the inclusion of a JPG/JPEG image at the top and a GIF image as the button that can be clicked to return to the home page, as well as locations of the linked files. You can view the HTML underlying a page on the Internet by going to the View menu and selecting Document Source or a similar command.

Sample of Hypertext Markup Language (HTML)

```
<!DOCTYPE HTML PUBLIC "-//W3C//DTD HTML 3.2//EN">
<HTML>
<HEAD>
    <TITLE>Career</TITLE>
    <META NAME="Author" CONTENT="ehy">
    <META NAME="GENERATOR" CONTENT="User-Agent: Mozilla/3.0Gold (Macintosh; I; PPC)">
</HEAD>
<BODY>
<CENTER><TABLE CELLSPACING=2 CELLPADDING=2 >
<TR>
<TD><IMG SRC="LIZ.JPG" HEIGHT=100 WIDTH=100 ALIGN=LEFT></TD>

<TD><B><I><FONT SIZE=+1>Career Highlights</FONT></I></B></TD>
</TR>
</TABLE></CENTER>

<UL>
<LI>Founder of <A HREF="../../../../WACE09/HOME.HTM">women @the cutting edge</A> a project to
celebrate achievements through developing professional portfolios while training staff in the use of
technology </LI>

<LI>Developed <A HREF="Liz%20Archive/mock cv">Graduate Mentor Program</A>for Institution of
Engineers, 1998 </LI>

<LI>Developed <A HREF="Liz%20Archive/mock cv">Women in Leadership</A>, Mentoring and
Managing Diversity programs for the Department of Education 1996-8</LI>

<LI>Developed and delivered successful two day leadership programs for the <A HREF="../../../../
LLog1 ">Australian Principals Center</A> 1996-9 </LI>

<LI>Edited the 60 page <A HREF="../../../../Port">Leadership Log</A> for the Australian
Principals Center 1996</LI>

<LI>Initiated and developed an accredited short course <A HREF="Liz%20Archive/mock
cv">Creating the Learning Organization</A></LI>

<LI>Produced <A HREF="portcover">Professional Development for Educational Leadership</
A>: a statewide strategy plan for professional development for school leaders</LI>

<CENTER><TABLE BORDER=2 CELLSPACING=2 CELLPADDING=2 BGCOLOR=
"#89F08A" >
<TR>
<TD><IMG SRC="GIF%20aqua%20arrow" HEIGHT=26 WIDTH=26></TD>

<TD>
<UL>
<P><B><FONT SIZE=+1>Return to home page</FONT></B></P>
</UL>
</TD>
</TR>
</TABLE></CENTER>
```

FIGURE 4.4

The need for learning hypertext markup language has been diminished because most current software has the ability to save or convert files to HTML as a standard option.

8. Writing an Introduction for Each Element

The elements—competencies, standards, or criteria—chosen to make up the framework of the portfolio should each have a written introduction. The next stage of the portfolio development process is to write a brief statement about each artifact, providing a context for the reader and explaining how the artifact demonstrates evidence. Following is an introduction to the artifact shown in Figure 2.3 (Chapter 2) in which the teacher explains why she teaches as she does and how the artifact, which is a text, graphics, and sound file, demonstrates her teaching philosophy.

> "My students are encouraged to submit projects for assessment in the way that they believe best suits the topic. This example of a Music project about rock groups required students to present a report that compared the music of their selected rock group (in this case the Beatles) with another group or singer. One student who was learning Visual Basic in Information Technology class created an interactive multimedia presentation that incorporated graphics, sound and text to provide a more interesting and more effective report than a print document.
>
> The artifact represents my innovative teaching style and my encouragement of students to demonstrate their knowledge and understanding in ways suited to them. This illustrates acknowledgement of Gardner's theory of the multiple intelligences and the desirability of allowing and encouraging students to utilize the range in their learning and demonstration of learning. Producing this presentation required the student to really listen to the music of two different musical performers and analyze it carefully. He had to select excerpts from recordings of the performers' music that not only differentiated their music styles but demonstrated the qualities of each style. The final product was of much greater quality than I could receive from students who used print media to present their projects" (Taylor 1997).

In another example, a claim related to an outcome might include a statement such as the one that follows. This example comes from the draft guidelines for university staff and is related to the topic 'Coping strategies':

> "The evidence I have submitted illustrates my particular approach to coping with the pressures of the job. I am not easily stressed by things

> that are within my own control: for example, I found planning and writing my first term's teaching material hard work but very satisfying. I was lucky because I had a lot of material from my PhD which I could draw on directly! But I have found that the unexpected demand to fit in another seminar group and develop a course in an area that is fairly new to me has caused great pressure.
>
> The documents that I attach as evidence show the steps I took to discuss this with the Course Tutor and a colleague who has been particularly helpful. I have also included the planner that I used as a discipline and an incentive to get the extra work ready on time" (D. Baume, personal communication, June 9, 1998).

Without such a statement, the reader might not see the apparent links between the evidence and the element in question. Making a statement about the context, objectives, and purposes as an introduction or claim helps to make these apparent. Each artifact should be accompanied by a brief statement or caption which describes the context in which it was created as well as identifying details. The examples above demonstrate that this can be done in one or two brief paragraphs. It is not an arduous task.

Permission to Use Artifacts

It is essential to gain permission to reproduce, quote, or refer to the work of others. This is not only a courtesy, but also a way of further verifying the source of the data and remaining ethical in the presentation of artifacts. It is wise to seek permission to reproduce student work, no matter the ages of the students.

9. Reflecting on Each Element

Reflection, as described in Chapter 3, is a very important part of the learning process. Thus, it should be an aspect of every portfolio. Reflective commentaries do more than describe the artifacts and their context; they examine the knowledge, skills, attitudes, and values of the portfolio developer.

In the following example, a teacher reflects on her role in the school's triennial review process:

> "Although I have provided leadership in a range of areas including managing projects, curriculum development and staff welfare matters, this artifact represents my most recent and in some ways most challenging role in that I had to draw on a range of communications skills (to

> persuade, cajole, resolve conflict, gain consensus), analytical skills to interpret and comment about the data gathered during the process, and project management skills to develop and meet timelines.
>
> On reflection, I would have preferred for staff to have more time to analyze the data rather than to discuss an analysis I presented to them. This would have encouraged deeper debate and discussion of educational issues than did occur. The Principal agreed to allocate more time to charter development at staff meetings and Professional Development meetings and we had a longer timeline so I was able to provide more time for debate when we moved into the phase of new charter development. Additional personal Professional Development I undertook in communication skills also gave me some additional tools to use to encourage staff input and I am now confident the quality of the new charter will reflect the more active input of staff, Council and students and thus be more representative of a collective view" (Taylor 1997).

This example demonstrates the ways that the teacher works as a leader in her school and what she has learned from the review process. The inclusion of reflective writing provides more than a catalog of achievements—it provides rich information about the teacher's values and goals.

10. Reflecting on Vision and Values

While this step appears to be last in the list, it is the key to the ongoing nature of the portfolio approach, as the growth demonstrated and the achievements highlighted are now reconsidered. Reflection aids in making portfolio production a recursive process.

Mary Diez (1996) reminds us that the portfolio encourages reflection in at least three different ways. It provides the freedom and discipline to identify a structure that views or presents one's own work, provides the opportunity to assess one's strengths and weaknesses by careful examination of the artifacts used to meet the specified framework, and leads to professional goal setting for the future through self-assessment and reflection.

The portfolio also gives teachers an opportunity to communicate their values. A principal writes about focusing her values and vision after reflecting on the evidence of professional growth and achievement she has presented:

> "Leadership—my leadership changed from being internal to external. People saw what I did. I planted seeds. I challenged the process. I nurtured and supported my people throughout our journey. We could not have made the gains we did had I not done this. Stephen Covey's

"law of the farm" remained firmly implanted in my mind. I have also always believed that people themselves are the leaders. I try to make sure that I am but the lead-follower. I try to give people the tools to strengthen their roots, so they develop strong wings, to fly to become leaders themselves. And this has happened.

- Quality—we often talked about this, but now we looked at every aspect of our work with students and with each other and asked the question. 'Was this the quality we wanted?' If not, we improved it. Continuous quality improvement became lived actions, with all of us.

- Systems focus—we began to focus on the big picture and develop an understanding of the parts. This helped all of us to understand the complexities that exist with each issue. It also helped us to appreciate chaos and to see the patterns within.

- Change—when addressing any new issue, the aspect of change is well thought out.

Personal Mastery became our focus for living our beliefs about lifelong learning.

- Community—we moved from collaboration, from team-building to ensuring that our goal was always towards building community, with all our stakeholders.

- Commitment—all staff became committed to our vision and mission, even to the point of developing vision and mission statements of their own.

- Working from the heart, inspiring others—I had always been doing this, or so I felt. Now, I made a point of making sure this was part of each of my day's work" (McLean 1998, p. 5).

This type of reflection can take the form of an essay that is placed in the Personal Archive, to be incorporated into a portfolio as an artifact, as outlined in Chapter 3. In later years, it might be drawn upon to show professional growth.

At this point, the portfolio developer has produced a record that clearly displays values, vision, achievements, and reflection, and in doing so, has had the opportunity to review aspects of teaching and leadership. The physical size of this record will be quite substantial if it is not in digital form. As each year goes by, and another portfolio is required, teachers and administrators are likely to opt for the digital version, which can be viewed via the Internet, recorded on CD-ROM, or shown on a laptop computer.

These ten steps form the basis of the portfolio development process. Without continual reflection on vision and values, updating the Personal Archive, and awareness of new purposes and contexts, portfolio development could become just another production line. In Chapters 5 and 6 we see how using multimedia technology can assist in producing a dynamic, living portfolio.

Chapter 5

The Technological Aspects of Digital Portfolios

"It [producing a multimedia portfolio] is really simple when you know how! The possibilities seem endless, only limited by our imagination."

—Grilanc, personal communication,
January 18, 1999

Once you have developed your Personal Archive and have followed the steps in Chapter 4 for preparing your portfolio, you are ready to decide which multimedia method is best suited for presentation of your portfolio to your audience. This chapter describes the range of technologies that can be used to produce and present a digital portfolio. You will learn how to store artifacts and make them available for others to view.

Determining Your Audience

Before deciding on the best form of presentation for the portfolio, it is important to determine the audience and their familiarity with the technology. As discussed in Chapter 1, the purpose of the portfolio determines both its audience and its structure. When the time comes to select items from the Personal Archive to create a portfolio, these two areas must be considered. The audience might include:

- colleagues
- supervisors
- a school community
- a selection panel in another school or organization
- prospective employers
- Internet surfers around the world

Once you know the nature of the audience, it is important to find out whether they are prepared for the type of portfolio you plan to produce. For example, will they be able to read a CD-ROM or access the Internet? A living portfolio is a portfolio that can be easily modified by the author and easily read by the audience. Multimedia is a vehicle that allows for this type of flexibility, and the level of sophistication used will be determined in part by the audience's capacity to access the technology. Once you have determined the necessary information about the audience, you can decide which format to use for portfolio presentation.

How to Present Your Digital Portfolio

There are several options for the presentation of a multimedia portfolio. Educators can take a laptop computer to a discussion or interview in the same way they would take a portfolio in a binder. When the portfolio is designed to stand alone without further explanation, educators can make copies on CD-ROM and mail them to the selected audience, or they can put the portfolio on the Internet. These formats use much less physical space than the binder portfolio, and the educator who has produced such a portfolio can create a very impressive image.

In her book, Cynthia Baron (1996) describes the technical aspects of producing a multimedia portfolio for visual artists, designed particularly as a marketing tool. These methods easily apply to educators who wish to record and present information in digital form, and the basic steps are described in this chapter. Contrary to what is often believed, it is possible to produce simple, attractive documents without the latest high-tech equipment, using commonly available software. As discussed, there are various ways to store and present a digital portfolio. A few of these methods are described below.

CD-ROM

A small portfolio might fit on a floppy disk, but when the file takes up more space because graphics, sound, and video have been incorporated, it can be saved onto a CD-ROM. Blank CDs for recording, called "rewritable CDs" and "recordable CDs" can be bought at many of the same places where floppy disks are sold. Most new computers sold today contain CD-ROM drives which are able to read a CD-ROM. Access to this type of basic hardware is becoming more widespread for both the portfolio producer and the audience. However, remember to make sure that your audience has access to a CD-ROM drive if you plan to present your portfolio this way.

Laptop Computer

A laptop computer is an ideal place to store the portfolio if you want to control the presentation. The usable memory on laptops nowadays is quite large, allowing for graphics, sound, and video to be saved. For presentation to very small groups, the laptop screen may be sufficient, and for larger groups the presentation can be shown via a data projector attached to the computer, with the image projected onto a large screen. Laptop computers can be easily transported to conferences, meetings, and interviews, and they make it very easy to update material.

The Internet

The Internet enables the widespread transmission of information in a range of multimedia formats including text, sound, animation, and video. A portfolio home page can be easily accessed through a browser such as Netscape Navigator™ or Microsoft Internet Explorer™ and is potentially available to all users of the Internet worldwide. Users may read, copy, and print the pages.

Creating a portfolio for distribution on the Internet is similar to creating a CD-ROM, but the audience is wider. It is possible to load the portfolio onto the Internet and maintain some control over access by giving out the address or URL (Uniform Resource Locator) only to selected audiences. (Reference "Publishing Your Portfolio" in Chapter 6, pages 75–78,, for more information on how to load your portfolio and create a URL.) If your portfolio is intended for a wide audience to make contact with employers, researchers, or like-minded colleagues, it can be registered with search engines such as Yahoo™ and Altavista™. To register, refer to the Internet home page of the search engine (for example, www.altavista.com) and follow the instructions. There are various ways that the producer can retain control over which material is made publicly available.

When communicating with the audience, the multimedia producer also needs to remember that the browsers used to access the Internet differ. This means that the same document can appear differently to individual users. Even with the same browser the "preferences" setting can be changed due to individual controls for font, text size, and color, so it is difficult to predict how the pages will be seen, although the basic information will certainly be displayed. The size of the window can also be adjusted, so the layout of the pages can also appear differently. In summary, Figure 5.1 shows which aspects of the multimedia portfolio presentation are in the control of the producer and which are in the control of the reader.

FIGURE 5.1

Producer and Reader Control of Multimedia Presentation

Producer's Control	*Reader's Control*
• Laptop and personal presentation • CD posted to selected employers • URL (on Internet) restricted	• Internet open access; search engines notified • Layout, text, font preferences

How to Store Material in Digital Form

In recent years there has been a great deal of interest in commercial multimedia products on CD-ROM, which are often used to store games, encyclopedias, and software because their capacity is greater than that of the floppy disk. However, teachers and administrators are often surprised to learn that many schools already have the equipment required to create a basic multimedia portfolio, and some even have a CD writer to store it on CD-ROM. The hardware and software items needed to produce a digital portfolio are described in the following pages.

A dynamic living portfolio can be created using images, sound, and video clips to display evidence of a teacher's work. Any photograph, diagram, or even hand-written letter contained in a Personal Archive can be scanned into a word document to show information. Audio- and videotapes can capture teachers in action or record student presentations or speeches. This material can be stored in digitized form on floppy disk, creating a catalog of evidence comprised of text, sound, graphic or video files. Some simple methods of storing graphic and sound material efficiently are described below.

Scanning

There is no need to retype printed documents. Papers or selections from documents can be scanned using a scanner attached to a computer (as shown in Figure 5.2) with software such as Omnipage™. After a text document is scanned it will appear as a word processing document and can be edited as needed. Scanning software that can be installed on your computer is usually sold with scanners. The scanning program will then display instructions for scanning on your computer screen. Documents can be scanned almost as easily as they can be photocopied. Some common software programs are Microsoft PhotoEditor™ (in Microsoft Office™), Adobe Photoshop™, and CorelDraw™. When scanning hand-written letters, cards, or photographs, use the software's image editor and follow the instructions, and the documents will be stored as image files that can be inserted into other documents. Scanned documents are able to be stored on a computer disk for use as required.

FIGURE 5.2

Photographs

Any camera can be used to take photographs of the teacher and students engaged in activities, or of projects or assignments being implemented. It is very useful to keep a camera on hand in the classroom to record highlights and to encourage students to observe opportunities for recording.

Photos that are part of the Personal Archive can be scanned into digital format using a scanner, such as the one pictured above. The images then can be stored on disk and imported into documents as required. (Importing photos is explained in more detail in Chapter 6, page 69.) If there is no scanner available in the school, photographs can be taken to printing or imaging agencies to be scanned. Some libraries may also have scanning capabilities. Drawings, paintings, and newspaper articles can also be scanned or photographed.

The scanning program provides options for saving images at various resolutions, measured in dots per inch (dpi) or pixels. Graphics to be used on the Internet are usually saved at a lower resolution than those prepared for printing. The person scanning the image can adjust the resolution as appropriate. Graphics are best saved as GIF or JPG/JPEG files if they are intended for use on the Internet. This can be done by selecting the GIF or JPG/JPEG option under the Save As menu. Adobe Photoshop™ is a program that can be used to adjust the color, contrast, and other aspects of the image if necessary.

Digital Photographs

Digital cameras are becoming more common as a means of photographing directly to disk rather than to film, thereby saving time. Images can be downloaded from the disk to the computer for use in documents. Images to be stored in the Personal Archive need to be clearly identified with the date, event, names, and any other useful information to allow for easy access during the production process.

Videotaping

Many teachers and their students have made videotapes of students' classroom activities or created videotapes for classroom use. Some presentations or activities are best communicated through visual and verbal information, making the videotape the perfect medium. Coaches have used videotape for many years to identify strengths and weaknesses and to record change over time. Sometimes a few minutes of tape are enough to assist a teacher in the quest for self-awareness and to suggest areas for development. Videotapes also can be used by groups of teachers to record meetings or prepare videotaped lessons for wider audiences. Archived videotapes should be clearly labeled with the date, event, and school for future reference.

Video can be stored digitally by using a video capture card and appropriate software in the computer. Replay your video on a player connected to your computer and follow the instructions to select the clips you want to save. Video can then be stored digitally on a disk as part of your Personal Archive. Give these clips appropriate file names as you save them. To play video clips you need a program such as Quicktime™ or RealAudio/Video™. If your computer does not have this software installed you can download it from the Internet.

Audio

Many forms of sound can be readily recorded for the portfolio by using an audiocassette with a portable recorder. In addition, many computers can record sound through a small microphone if they have the correct software and a sound card, which most computers now come supplied with. The computer microphone works similarly to a tape recorder, and the instructions for use are shown on the screen. Saving sound files to disk is just like saving text or video files to disk.

For higher-quality sound, audiocassettes can be transferred to digital mode. To achieve higher-quality sound, a Digital Audio Tape (DAT) recorder can be used. DAT recorders produce the highest quality by recording directly in digital format to tape. The recording can then be transferred to the computer via the sound card inputs. Whatever the format selected for recording, improvements can be made by using a high quality microphone. For example, students might be taped giving class presentations, performing a musical composition, or singing in various languages. Teachers also might want to record themselves presenting papers at conferences or to a group as a way of reviewing and documenting their communication skills.

Text, graphics, sound, and video are the basic elements of multimedia. They can all be saved digitally to disk. Graphics, sound, and video files take up more space than text and can take a long time to access. It is wise to use highlights rather than the complete record when compiling a portfolio. Once teachers have gained experience in these areas, they will have options for production of portfolios, classroom materials, or presentations. A summary of suitable hardware and software for these purposes and their uses is found in Figures 5.3 and 5.4 (on the following pages).

The manuals that accompany the software programs mentioned in Figure 5.4 provide detailed advice about their use. Additional information and programs are available on the Internet or through any reputable computer supplier.

Once you have converted all the artifacts to be included in your multimedia portfolio to digital storage, you are ready to begin putting together the portfolio itself. Chapter 6 explains how to start and complete this process.

Common Hardware and Its Uses

Hardware and Equipment	*Uses*
computer (desktop or laptop)	too numerous to list!
camera	photographs, activities, documents, buildings, etc.
digital camera	photographs are converted directly to electronic form and stored on disk
scanner	converts printed documents and images to digital form
modem (internal or external to computer)	forms connections to telephone line for Internet access
video camera	records moving images
sound recorder	records sound
computer with sound card and internal or external microphone	records sound in digital format
computer with video adapter card and capture software	plays video recording on computer
CD Writer	stores large amounts of material on CD-ROM
computer with CD reader	reads CD-ROM
high density floppy (Zip™ disk)	stores 100MB of data on a 3.5″ disk
high density cartridge (Jaz™ disk)	stores 1GB of data on a removable cartridge
data projector	connects to computer to display images or text on a large screen

FIGURE 5.3

Software Suitable for Multimedia Production

Computer Software	*Uses*
MS Word™	word processing; version 7.0 and above can convert documents to HTML
MS Powerpoint™	creates slide shows; version 4.0 and above can convert documents to HTML
optical character recognition software such as Omnipage™	converts printed documents to digital form for word processing
image scanning software such as Vistascan™	converts images to digital form (preferably JPG/JPEG or GIF)
video capture software	creates digital video files
relational data bases, such as Filemaker Pro 4.0™	allow artifacts to be categorized by field
hypermedia "card" formats, such as HyperStudio™, HyperCard™, Digital Chisel™, SuperLink+™	allow for linking of cards by navigation tool
Adobe Acrobat™ (Portable Document Format)	allows documents to be read in their original format rather than HTML
Internet browser software such as Netscape Navigator™, Microsoft Explorer™	enables documents in HTML format to be read on the Internet
HTML editor software such as Netscape Composer™, Adobe Page Mill™, or Microsoft Front Page™	allows the creation (authoring) of HTML documents for the Internet and CD-ROM
Multimedia authoring software, such as Macromedia Authorware™, Macromedia Dreamweaver™, Macromedia Director™	allows more sophisticated authoring of HTML documents, including animation
Connection to Internet via Internet Service Provider (ISP)	publishes material on Internet

FIGURE 5.4

Chapter 6

A Living Portfolio

"A living portfolio is . . . an artistic event that calls for teachers to skillfully present their work and communicate their talents to others. The presentation allows for the work to stay alive."
—Morriss, personal communication, January 12, 1999

Teachers and administrators who are in a constant state of growth benefit most from being represented by portfolios which are able to change constantly, portfolios which are living. Simple production methods can be executed to ensure high-quality, multifaceted, and effective professional portfolios. Chapter 4 demonstrated how the various elements of the portfolio must be planned and a concept map prepared for production of a digital portfolio. This chapter shows how to create a set of linked materials for an element in a portfolio that will be placed on the Web. These guidelines assume that the material selected from the Personal Archive is now in a variety of digital formats, such as text, image, sound, and video files, as explained in Chapter 5.

Developing a Plan for Your Portfolio

Portfolio preparation is assisted by establishing a well-organized Personal Archive, as described in Chapter 3. When producing a new portfolio for a particular purpose, it is important to make a list of the head ings, or elements, to be used for the structure, and then to write down everything which should be included under those headings. This will indicate places where there are gaps in the material or places where there is too much material. It is a good idea to organize this list on sticky notes, as this allows elements to be rearranged until a logical design is achieved.

Next, the chosen artifacts are taken from the archive. If they are in digital form, they can be transferred into a new folder named "Portfolio" to ensure they can be easily found and incorporated into the new portfolio. If the artifacts are not yet digital, they need to be transferred into a digital format as described in Chapter 5, pages 58–61.

It is very helpful to decide on a system of consistent and logical file names for a digital portfolio. Some teachers use a consistent prefix for each file relating to a particular element, such as leadership. The name of each file relating to this element might then begin with the letters "lead." Once production has started, it becomes very time-consuming to change file names, as all the links to a page in the portfolio will have to be changed if the name of the file in which it is found is changed.

Templates can provide a helpful framework for planning your portfolio. These vary from a detailed database style to a set of headings or criteria with clear guidelines for entering material (Reiss 1998). Templates can also be created and adapted by educators to develop their own portfolio plan. There is a range of commercial portfolio software packages designed for use in student assessment that can also be used by teachers (Barrett 1998).

However, templates or portfolio software packages are not mandatory. The actual examples of multimedia portfolios used in this book are screen grabs of teachers' portfolios that are on the Internet. These teachers have created their own portfolio structures and used the web editing software associated with their Internet browsers to complete the portfolio. Through the use of video clips showing a class at work, photographs of curriculum publications, and evidence provided through text documents, these teachers have been able to effectively demonstrate their achievements. The text accompanying each artifact should include commentary and reflection. Time spent on preparation, production, and presentation ensures a high-quality outcome.

When planning your multimedia portfolio, it is important to begin with the end product in mind. Figure 6.1 (on the following page) includes helpful hints for creating an organized, efficient, and effective multimedia portfolio.

FIGURE 6.1

Tips for an Easy-to-Read Multimedia Portfolio

1. Organize the material carefully and design the site before starting production.
2. Provide informative headings that clearly indicate the content of sections.
3. Avoid large amounts of text on a page, and keep paragraphs brief. Get straight to the point.
4. Keep the lists of choices offered to the reader/audience to a minimum.
5. Make graphics, sound, and video files as small as possible, and use them sparingly—some audiences may not be able to access them.
6. Put navigation options and content headings near the top of the page where they are easy to find, as some users won't scroll all the way down the page to find information.
7. To ensure that readers focus on the content, limit the use of bold, capitals, italics, blinking text, multi-colors, and underlining. They can be distracting to the reader.
8. Write most of the material in the active voice.
9. Always back up your files and keep at least one copy of each.
10. Make the links worth visiting, i.e., make sure they contain relevant information.
11. Don't lose readers by offering them many external links to organizations that are not linked back to your website.
12. Make sure that each document does not require the reader to have read the preceding material: if the portfolio is on the Internet, search engines can access the site at any point, so the material needs to be able to stand alone.
13. If you are putting your portfolio on the Internet, provide an e-mail address in a hypertext and/or graphical link format. This will enable people to easily send messages and questions directly to you.
14. Record the dates of production and updating so the reader can see how current the information is.

Producing a Multimedia Portfolio

As noted previously, HTML (hypertext markup language) is the language that is used for writing pages for the Internet and creating links between documents. At this stage it is not necessary that your material be in HTML. Any web editor such as Netscape Navigator Gold™, Netscape Composer™, or an authoring program like Adobe Page Mill™ or Macromedia Dreamweaver™ will convert files from word processing programs into HTML. Microsoft Word 7.0™ can also be used to save documents directly to HTML.

These days it isn't necessary to know how to write in HTML to create web pages. An easy way to create a multimedia portfolio for distribution or display on CD-ROM and the Internet is to use a WYSIWYG (What You See Is What You Get) editor such as Netscape Gold™ or Netscape Composer™, which is included in Netscape Communicator™. These are related to browsers (software like Netscape Navigator™) that give you access to the World Wide Web. They allow for the production (editing) of web pages. Many browsers and editors are "cross-platform," which means that they operate on Windows and Macintosh platforms, so a portfolio can be created using either of these platforms.

Beginning Production

A screen such as the one shown below in Figure 6.2 appears when a web editor is first opened.

FIGURE 6.2

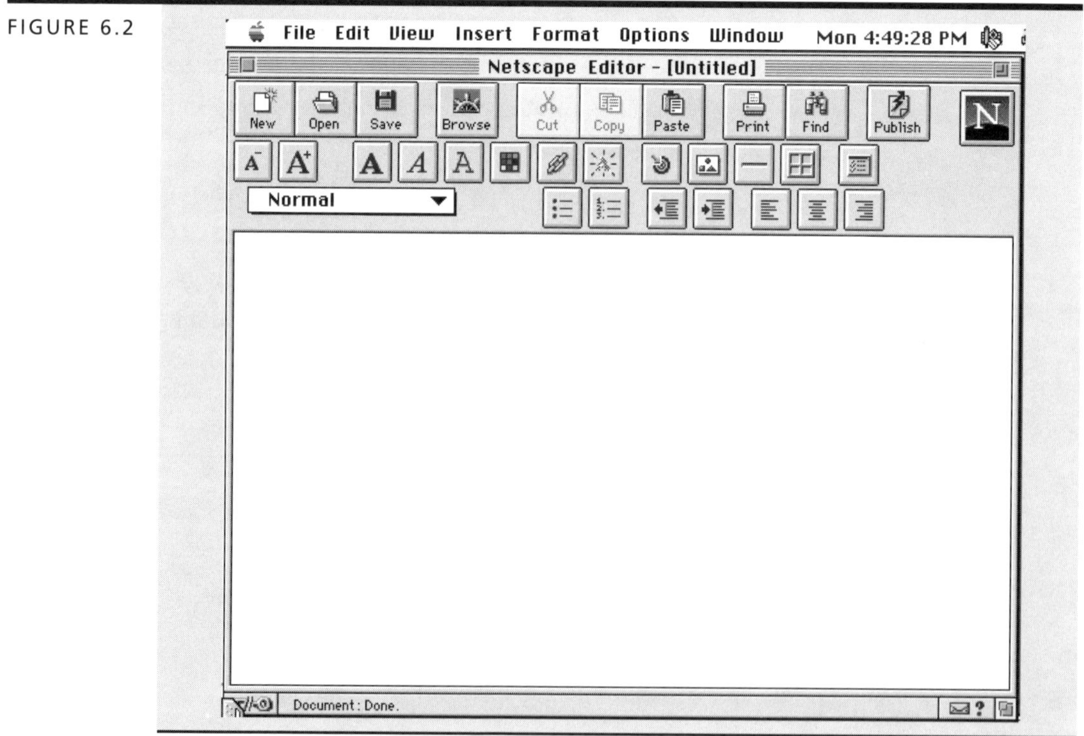

To begin creating your first page, you need to create a New Document under the File menu. This will provide you with a blank screen that you can type directly on or paste previously copied text from a word-processed file. This page should include your name as well as the purpose of the portfolio and the elements within it. You might want to include a photograph here.

One way to keep the page neat is to create a table in which to paste the various text items and photographs. This is done under the Insert menu, by clicking on the Table command and creating a table with, for example, two columns and two rows. You can then type the words "Professional portfolio" and your name in one cell, put your photograph in another cell, put the elements of the portfolio in the third cell, and use the fourth for a statement of purpose or philosophy, as shown in Figure 6.3. This first page can become the "home page" of a portfolio that is to be put on the Internet.

FIGURE 6.3

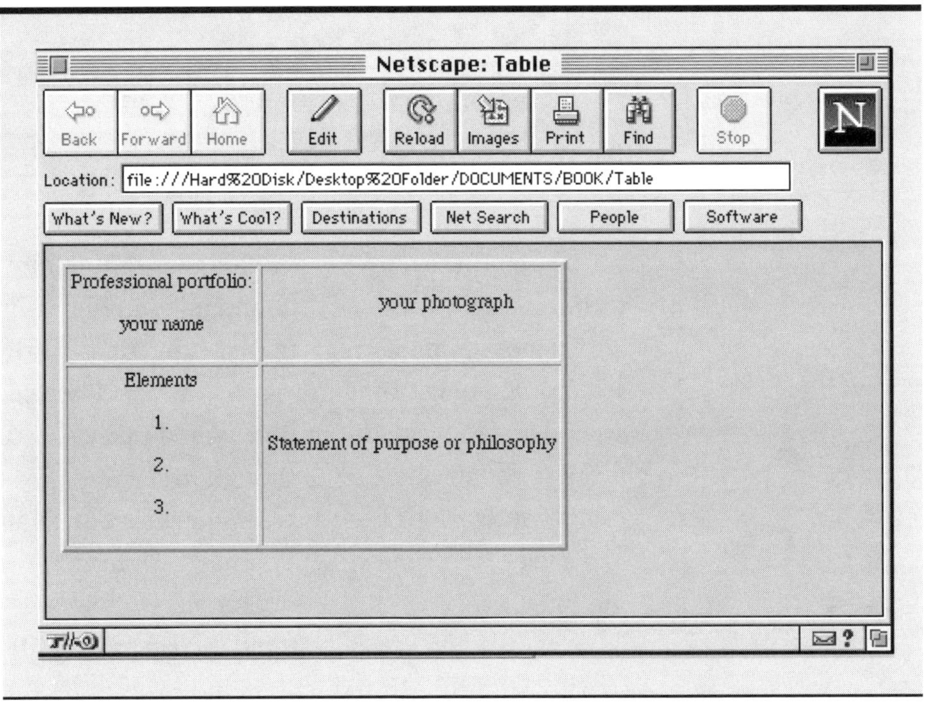

Netscape: Table

Back Forward Home Edit Reload Images Print Find Stop

Location: file:///Hard%20Disk/Desktop%20Folder/DOCUMENTS/BOOK/Table

What's New? What's Cool? Destinations Net Search People Software

Professional portfolio: your name	your photograph
Elements 1. 2. 3.	Statement of purpose or philosophy

To place your photograph (which is already saved as a GIF or JPG/JPEG file) in the table, place the cursor in the top right-hand cell of the table, choose the Insert menu and click on Image. Then choose the file name of your image and follow the instructions given by the computer. In Figure 6.4, on the following page, the name of the file containing the image to be inserted is "Maureen.JPG."

FIGURE 6.4

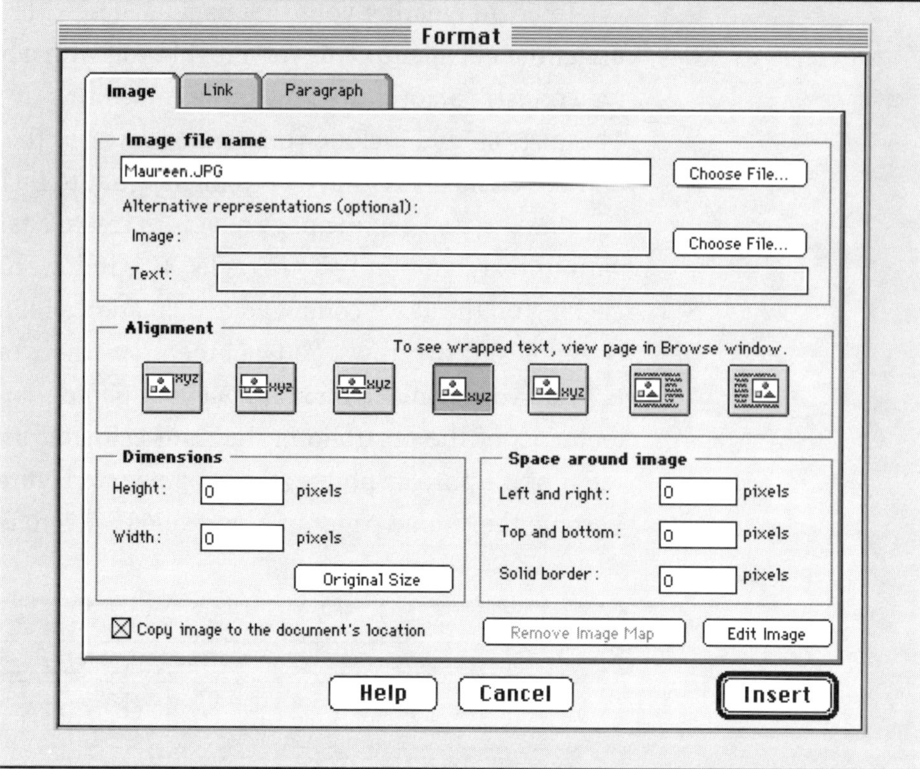

It's important to keep graphic files to a minimum, especially when the technological capacity of the intended audience is not known. Some sites with fancy graphics may take a long time to download on a computer screen. Download time from the Internet is two seconds per graphic + one second per K, so a 30K graphic would take 32 seconds to download under average conditions. 50K is thought to be the maximum size for this type of use if you want to keep your audience's attention. One minute can seem like a very long time when waiting for information to be downloaded from the Internet.

After placing any new items and saving the file, you can check the page by choosing the Browse command. The screen then appears as a reader might see it. You can make any necessary adjustments by reverting to the Edit command and making changes. Once video and sound files have been saved digitally, they can be placed in a similar manner. Select the place (text or image) where the video clip or sound is required and follow the Insert prompt to link the appropriate file. The reader can then choose whether to play the file or not.

It is important to follow your concept map when creating the documents in the portfolio. All the files that make up the text, graphics, etc., should be saved in folders on computer disks so that they can be easily retrieved.

Creating Links

The capacity to provide links between documents is one of the major attractions of a digital portfolio. Links are created quite easily by selecting the text on the page to be linked (in the example below it is "Learning and Development"), choosing the Insert menu, and then clicking on Link. (A click on the Link icon will have the same result.) When this is done, a screen such as that in Figure 6.5 will appear.

FIGURE 6.5

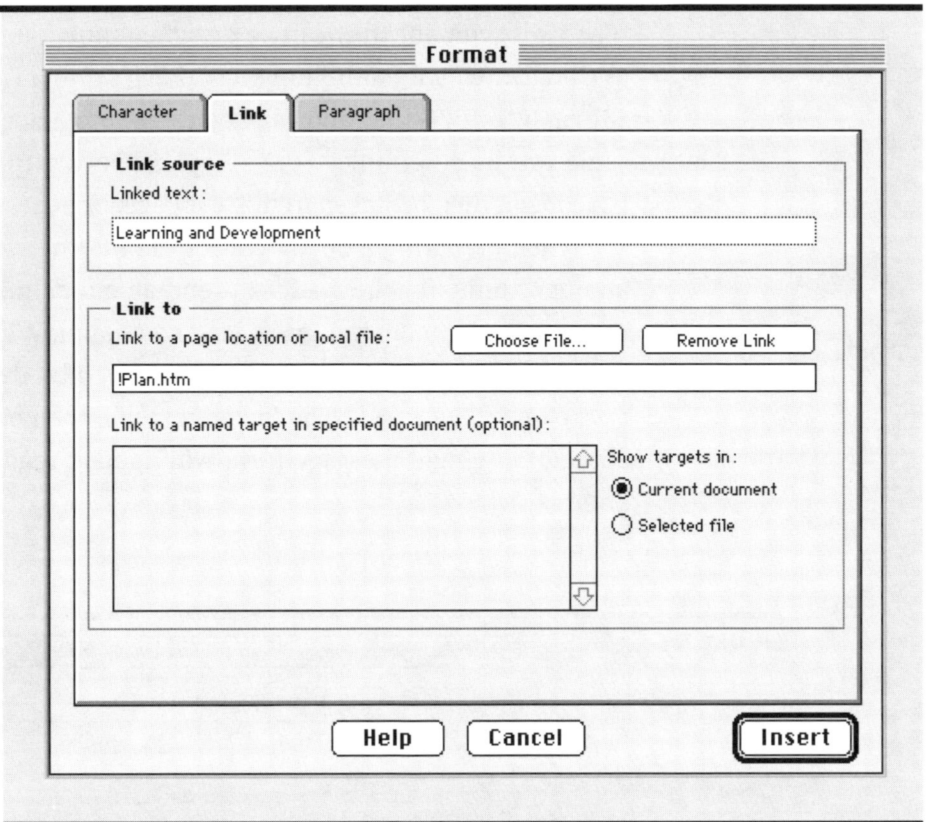

The computer screen will then ask you what file you want to link to. In this case "Learning and Development" is to be linked to another document, named "!Plan.htm." It also can be linked to a specific location in the document, such as to a text, image, or video clip. To do this, you must first select the desired Target in the file named Plan.htm. Whatever choice is made, a click on Insert will create the links between documents. The linked text will change color and will be underlined, indicating that it is now linked to further information, either in the same document, to another file in the portfolio, or even to a document on another website. Follow the same steps to link images, video, or audio to text.

Providing Navigation Symbols

One of the most important links is the text, icon, or button that takes the reader back to the home page or to preceding documents. Without links back, the reader can get lost. On each page, there should be an indicator telling the reader how to move on and how to return to the home page. These links are created as described above. Clear and consistent buttons or symbols, such as forward and backward arrows, should be provided to guide the reader. These can be downloaded from free graphics sites on the Internet, such as The Web Developer's Virtual Library at http://www.wdvl.com, or they can be designed individually using programs such as CorelDraw™ or PaintShop Pro™. Each symbol is an image file (such as a GIF or JPG/JPEG file) and can be pasted into a document and linked in the same way as other links. For example, a back arrow placed at the end of a page might then be linked to the first page, or home page, in your portfolio.

When preparing a document for the Internet, it is beneficial to include an opportunity for the reader to send an e-mail message back to you. This can be done through the Insert Link command. When asked what you wish to link to, type the words "mailto:" followed by the return e-mail address, as shown in Figure 6.6. The linked text will then be highlighted, and when clicked, an e-mail message form will appear, ready to send to the chosen address.

FIGURE 6.6

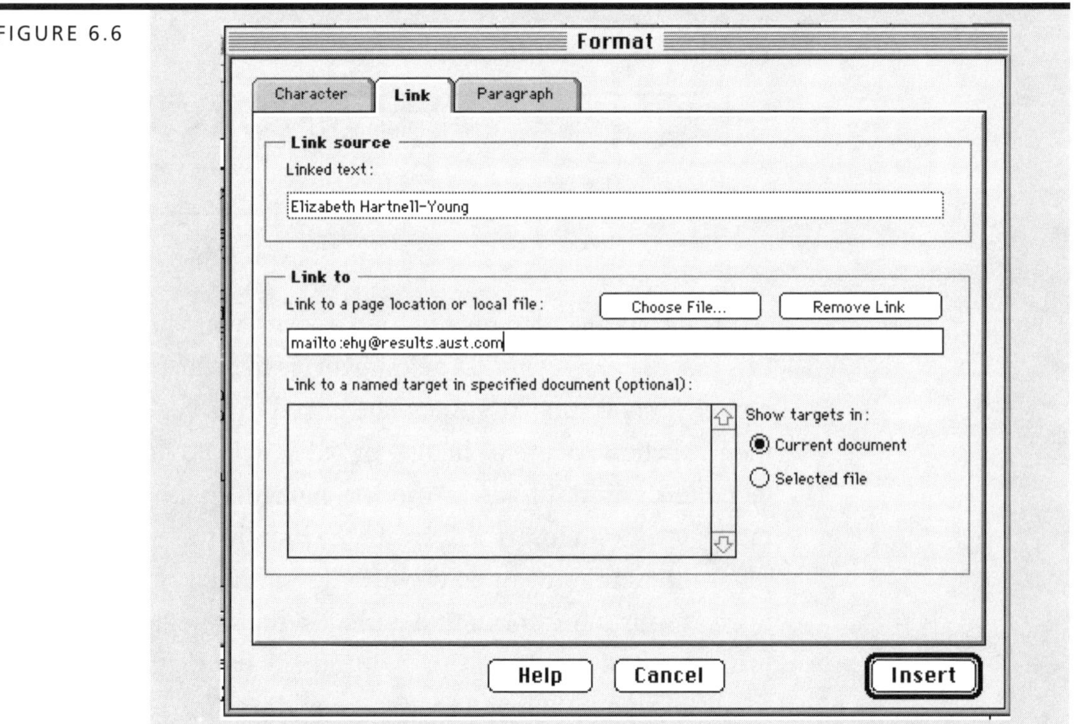

A Sample Portfolio

Elizabeth has been teaching for many years. She has decided to develop a multimedia portfolio to demonstrate her commitment to professional development for herself and others.

To help visualize the process described earlier, follow Elizabeth's journey as she puts together her multimedia portfolio. As Elizabeth creates her portfolio, each step will include all the information necessary to develop an effective and organized portfolio.

1. Elizabeth started her portfolio by collecting material about an industry placement she took as part of her professional development. This experience enabled her to learn more about the culture of a large multinational company. Her Personal Archive consists of evidence of the work she did in the company, including a photo taken with managers following the presentation of a report she wrote, a summary of the report, reflection on what she learned, and a few papers she wrote following the experience. She has selected these as the best artifacts from a much larger collection. The photograph has been scanned as a JPG/JPEG file, and the documents are all in Microsoft Word™. This means that all of Elizabeth's documents are now in a digital format.
2. Figure 6.7 (on the following page) shows a flowchart Elizabeth designed to illustrate how she wanted to link the material. Elizabeth created the pages to be short and informative and decided to use only one photograph to allow for easy loading for most Internet browsers. On each page she decided to include a button that links back to the first page in the section, and she also included a link to a website where one of her papers was published. Finally, to make sure that her readers would be able to contact her for further information or to ask questions, she created a link that included her e-mail address.
3. Once the links had been designed, the front page, or introduction, could be written. Using her word processing program, Elizabeth wrote her introduction and saved it as an HTML file. This "home page" could then be linked to other documents, including the element "Professional Development" in the following section.
4. Elizabeth used a web editor to prepare this section for her portfolio. She began by clicking on New Document (under the File menu). In order to keep the page neat and well-spaced, Elizabeth used the Insert menu and Table command to create a table with two columns and one row. She then typed the heading "Professional Develop-

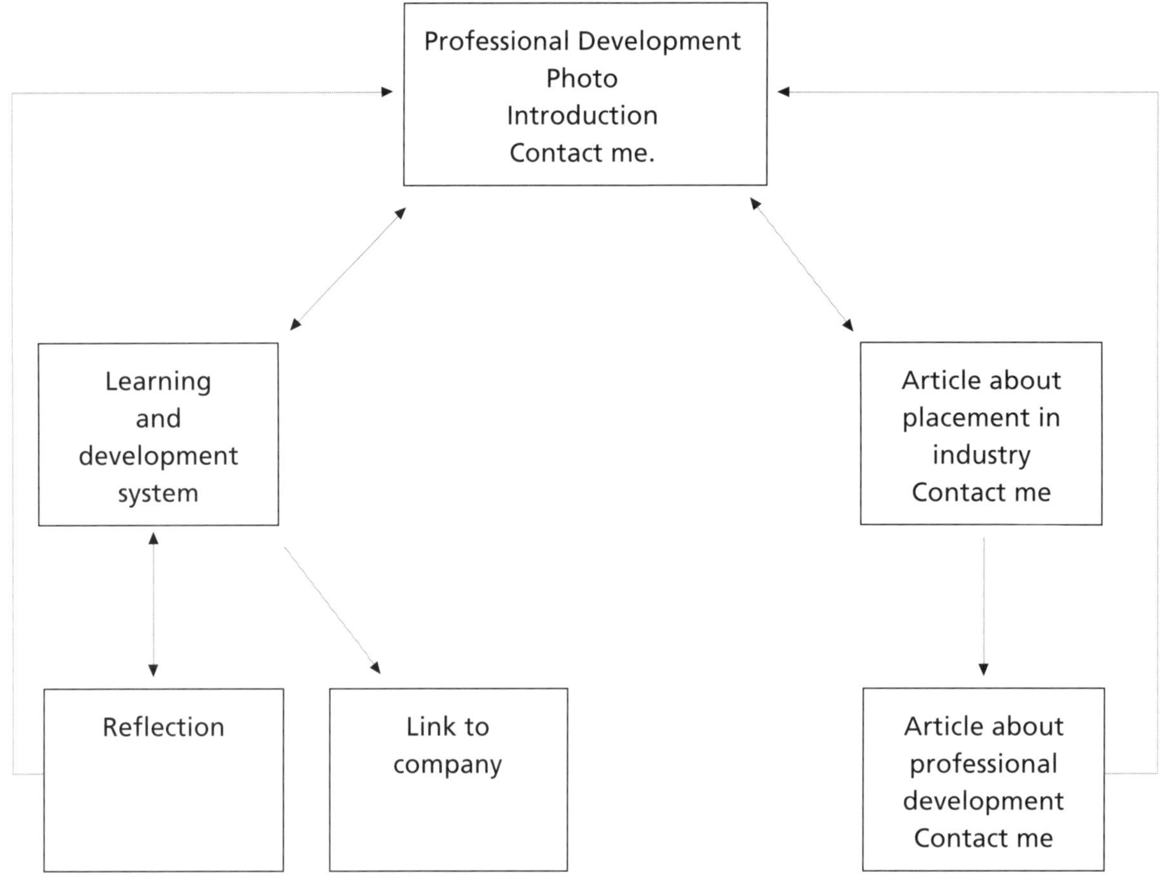

FIGURE 6.7

ment" in the left-hand column. She used the Insert menu to locate the JPG/JPEG file with the scanned image of her photograph, which she then inserted into the page. The size of the image was relatively small, 26K, so she knew it would not take her readers too long to load. The text accompanying the photo was copied from a word-processed document and pasted into the web editor. Figure 6.8 (on the next page) shows the resulting portfolio page.

FIGURE 6.8

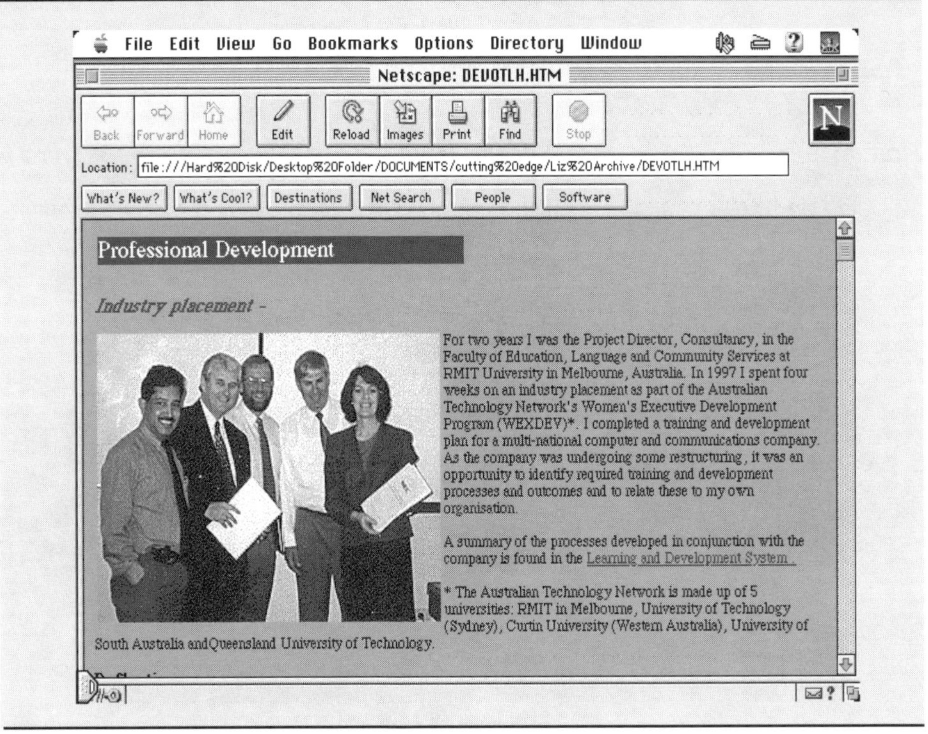

The only way to see the complete document is by scrolling down the page. However, the first link, shown here by underlined text, will be apparent. The link is engaged by clicking on the words "Learning and Development System," which have been highlighted and appear in a different color. Elizabeth created all the links in her portfolio by following the steps listed in "Creating Links" on page 71.

Figure 6.9, on the next page, shows the layout (including links) Elizabeth developed after creating and compiling her chosen elements.

This is just one example of providing links within an element. You can apply the same procedures to the other elements. The complete portfolio will then be introduced by a home page in the style of Figure 6.3 on page 69.

Publishing Your Portfolio

The completed portfolio can be shared with others in a variety of ways, as described in Chapter 5. You can decide which of the publishing or presentation formats listed on pages 77–78 best suits you and your audience before you begin the production process.

Contents of a Linked Element in a Digital Portfolio

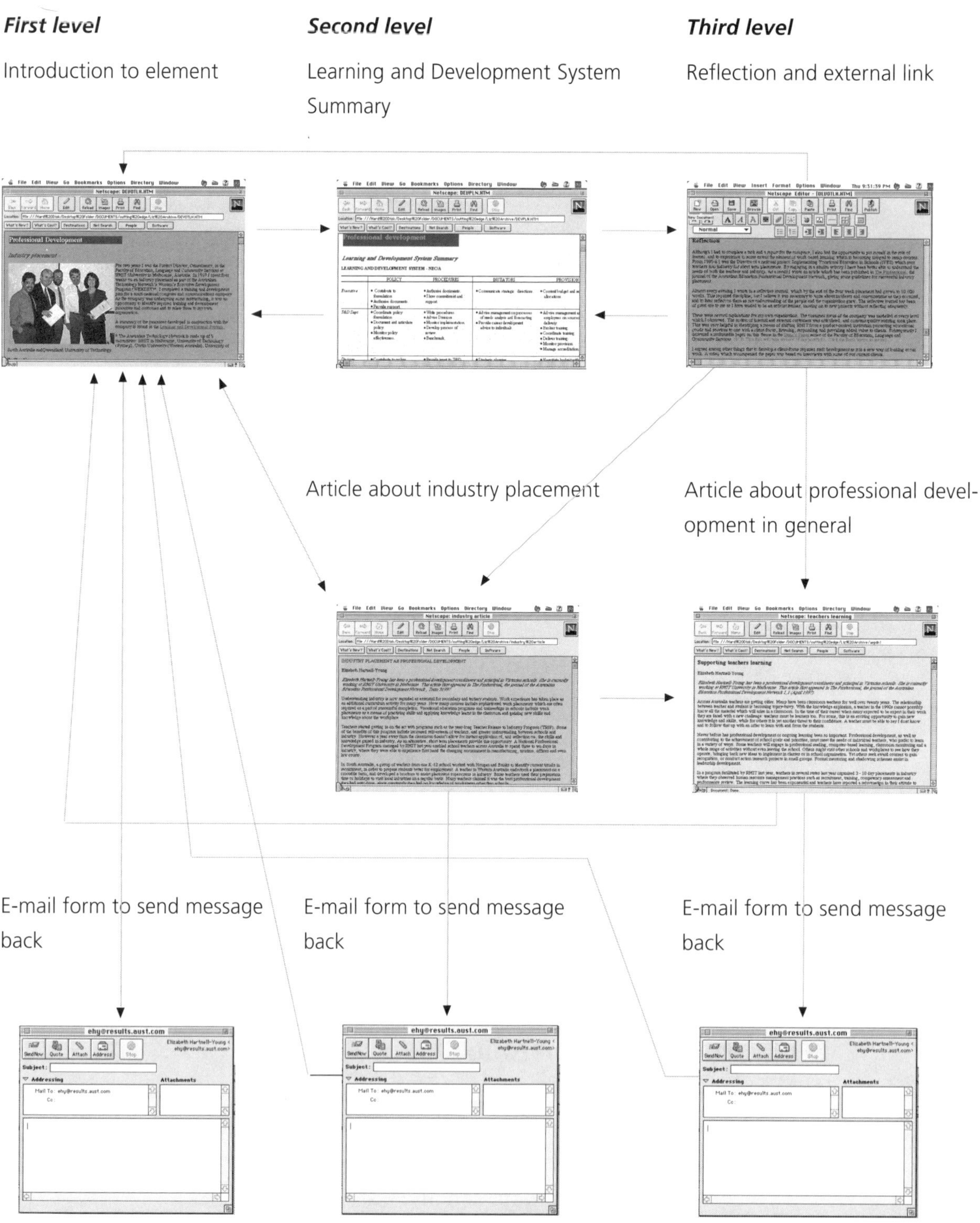

FIGURE 6.9

Writing the Portfolio to CD-ROM

As a multimedia portfolio will require a large amount of disk space, it may need to be saved to a CD-ROM using a CD authoring program and a CD-ROM writer (connected to the computer). In most cases, the authoring software is provided with the hardware. Most software is cross-platform, suitable for both Mac and PC. By following the instructions accompanying the CD-ROM writer, the actual transfer of files can progress systematically.

Publishing the Portfolio on the World Wide Web (www)

Once designed, files/pages need to be stored on a server to be accessible to Web users. Putting the files on a server is equivalent to publishing the document. To be able to do this, you need an Internet Service Provider (ISP). Most ISPs will provide instructions about publishing web documents. Schools or companies may already have an existing agreement with an ISP, and this ISP can inform you of your designated web address (URL).

The publishing process is relatively easy with most web authoring software. In the Publish command (shown in Figure 6.10) there is a space to type in the location information—a set of numbers—given by the ISP. Files can be transferred and published in a matter of minutes.

FIGURE 6.10

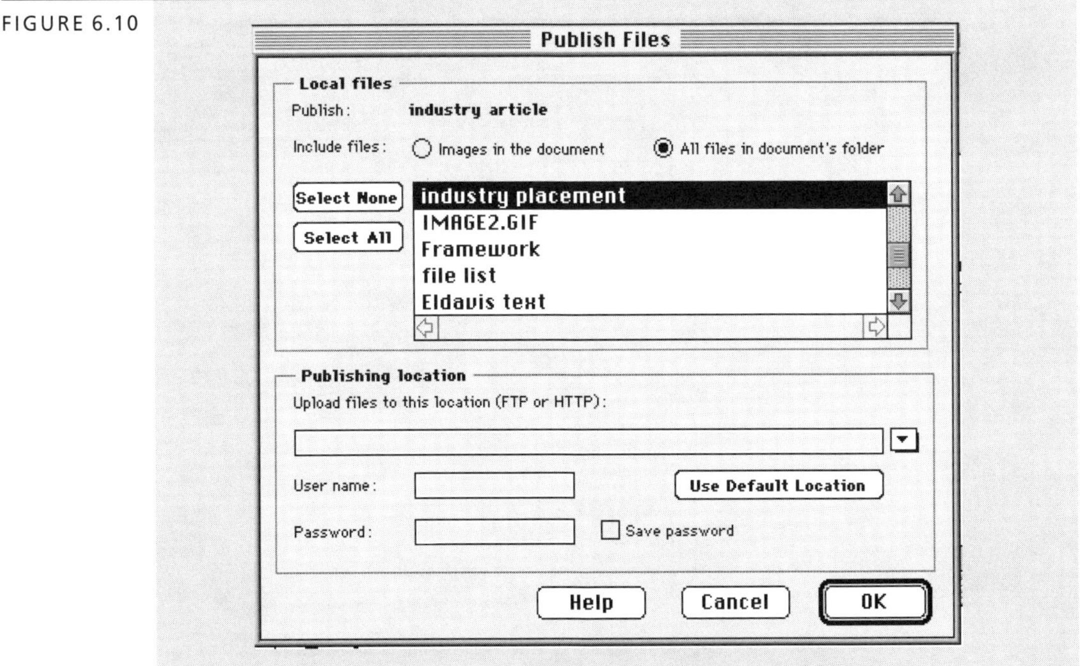

Laptop Computer

You might decide to save a copy of your portfolio to your laptop computer. In this case, the portfolio can be copied directly from a CD-ROM or from disks from your desktop to your laptop. You can even produce the portfolio directly on the laptop. Storing your portfolio on a laptop allows the portfolio to be updated very easily.

Developing Your Portfolio Further

For those who wish to develop their digital portfolio beyond the basics, there are more advanced options that can be implemented. These include some of the following techniques:

Color Schemes

Web editors provide simple ways to modify the color scheme of documents. This is done by opening a web editor, going into the Format menu, choosing Document and then clicking on Appearance, as shown in Figure 6.11. A range of colors that can be previewed for the background, text, and links will appear. When you have decided on your color scheme, click Apply, and the color will be applied to the chosen document.

FIGURE 6.11

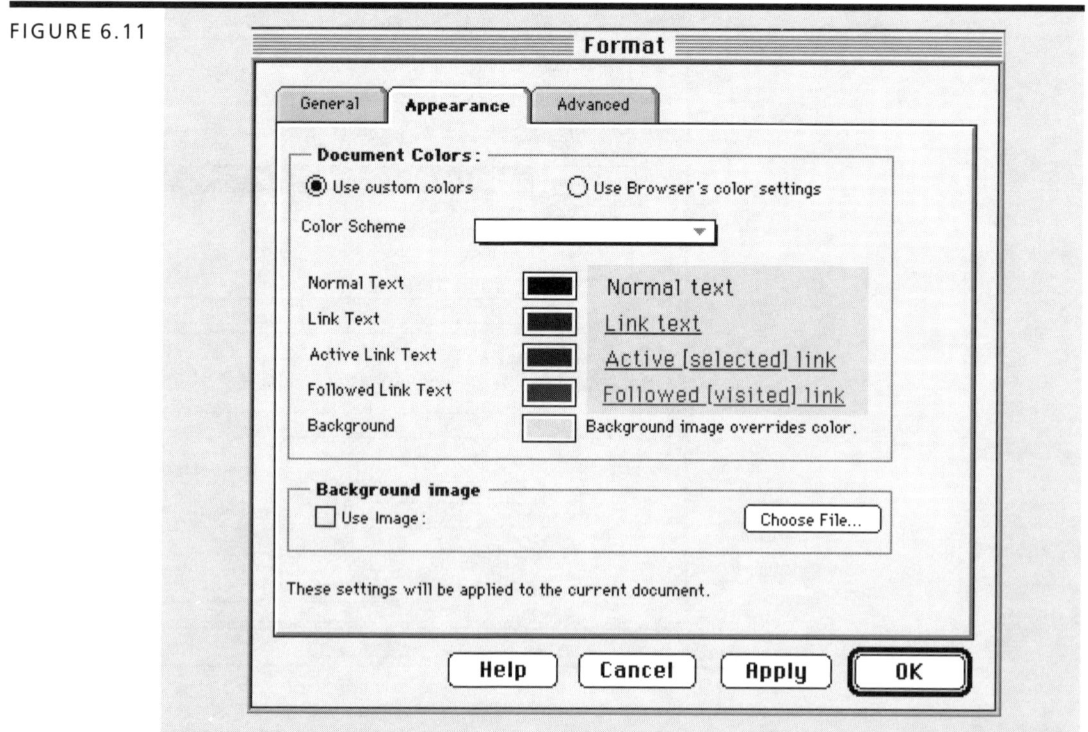

Using Image Maps

With image maps, different parts of an image, such as a map of the United States, a plan of the school, or a photograph of a group of people can be highlighted and linked to relevant information. Image maps do not work on all browsers, so they should be considered as an adjunct to the portfolio rather than an integral feature. A text-only equivalent of the information should be provided in case the user cannot access the image map. The steps in creating an image map are these:

- First, a GIF or JPG/JPEG formatted image is required, preferably with distinct sections to allow for zones to be created.
- Secondly, a map file, such as Mapedit™ for Windows or Webmap™ for Macintosh is required. A map file divides the image into discrete segments and uses a set of coordinates to label them.
- Finally, these labels are used to assign links from the various areas of the image to related documents in your portfolio. For example, the reader could click on an image map of school rooms and reach a linked page, containing perhaps an example of a class activity, a video clip, a reflection from the teacher, or any other relevant information. For those who wish to do further research on creating image maps, there are plenty of helpful hints in books (Lemay 1995) and on websites such as The Web Developer's Virtual Library (http://www.wdvl.com).

Creating Links to Other Relevant Sites

Sometimes a portfolio makes reference to work that has been commercially published, to previous employers, or to schools that have their own websites. In such cases, it can be useful to provide links to specific areas of other relevant sites. This is not a difficult process and can be done by following the Insert and Link commands previously described in Creating Links, page 71. However, it may be necessary to seek permission from the managers of the websites you plan to link to.

It is important to remember that while other sites have a great deal of interesting information, they may not have a way of linking back to the original portfolio. This means the reader could become lost and never get back to the original portfolio!

Copyright Issues

The wide availability of material on the web and the ability to copy text from web documents raises the important issue of copyrights. The author of the original work is clearly the copyright holder. Copyright laws indicate that any original work is protected even if there is not a notice to this effect in the document. It is a good idea to place a short copyright notice on each document you use in your portfolio. The copyright laws cover digital forms such as text, photographs, and audio files. If a photograph contains images of others, such as students, parents, or colleagues, a "model release"—a signed permission document—is required from each person shown in the image.

Portfolio developers need to be aware of the copyright laws and to err on the side of caution. There are sites that contain public domain materials that can be incorporated freely into new sites. However, as with any publication, it is always important to check the source of the material and verify that the material is indeed in the public domain.

Once you have finished developing your portfolio, it is a good idea to evaluate it to make sure it effectively communicates your goals. Rubrics and audience assessment guidelines are useful tools in portfolio evaluation. Chapter 7 contains information on these subjects as well as other important assessment tips.

Chapter 7

Evaluating a Multimedia Portfolio

"Portfolios, in conjunction with valid assessments, enable teachers to document their teaching in a way no other form of assessment can."

—Burke 1997, p. 121

We have described portfolio development as a process of professional growth that focuses on the individual at the center of the portfolio process. Evaluation of professional growth must reflect the person and not be distracted by, but rather assisted by, the presentation of the portfolio. This chapter provides suggestions for self-managed portfolio evaluation as well as rubrics that developers, supervisors, appraisers, or selection panels can use to evaluate portfolios.

Green and Smyser (1996) link the teacher's portfolio closely with education reform, arguing that many reform programs fail because they do not recognize that fundamental change in education does not occur without renewal and professional development of teachers. This approach requires a change in how teaching is assessed and how professional growth is guided. It is in this context that the focus must be on the purpose of portfolio development, remembering that it is a vehicle for individual growth that has the additional benefit of acting as a record for communication to others. The development of the portfolio is not the outcome. The outcome is improved student learning.

The assessment of professional portfolios is perhaps the most problematic issue in the portfolio development process. Assessment may not be an issue when the portfolio is used for formative purposes, such as for professional development, but it becomes more critical when used for promotion or performance review. Questions regarding assessment are often asked, such as: Who should assess the portfolio? What aspects of the portfolio are most important to consider during assessment? How will employers judge the value of a portfolio?

A portfolio which supports professional growth will first be evaluated by its producer, who reflects on the selection and presentation of material to decide if it meets the stated purpose and on the extent to which the ensuing portfolio truly represents and reflects the significance of the producer's work. Reflecting on the production of a multimedia portfolio also includes consideration of the technological skill development that occurred along the way and how this type of new knowledge can be shared with students and other teachers.

Assessing Your Portfolio

A portfolio for professional growth is clearly focused on the individual: her values, skills, knowledge, attitudes, and development. Thus, the individual must monitor and evaluate the material in the portfolio to ascertain that growth is represented. In this case, the portfolio acts as a videotape, rather than a single snapshot.

Wolf (1994) suggests that portfolio evaluators must possess sophisticated skills. They should be "individuals who (1) are very knowledgeable and experienced in the content, context and grade level being assessed, (2) represent a diversity of perspectives and backgrounds, and (3) are trained in the criteria and procedures for scoring the portfolio" (p. 132). These valuable attributes seem to reside within the producer and his peers. Therefore, for professional growth, it is important that the evaluation of all portfolios begins with the producer.

When evaluating a multimedia portfolio, there is a temptation to be dazzled by the presentation to the detriment of the content. A portfolio designed to record and display professional growth should include all three of the content areas covered in Chapter 4. These include:

- An introduction outlining purpose, values, and philosophy
- Artifacts displaying evidence consistent with the purpose, values, and philosophy
- Reflection on the evidence and on the learning and development displayed in the portfolio

Determining that the portfolio contains all three of the major content areas is the first step in portfolio evaluation. Once this is done, rubrics can be used to further evaluate your portfolio.

Rubrics for Portfolio Assessment

Rubrics are often developed by professional associations or by educational administrators. Rubrics developed to assist evaluation reflect the important aspects of a portfolio. Green and Smyser (1996) suggest that when portfolios are used to evaluate teachers, the rubrics should be developed in collaboration with the teachers themselves, while Brown and Irby (1997) report that this is in fact occurring in various school districts. Rubrics provide the portfolio developer with a checklist to consult while developing the portfolio. Figure 7.1, on the following page, contains generally applicable rubric guidelines that focus on the contents of a portfolio.

When the portfolio is being evaluated by someone other than the portfolio developer, it is important that the evaluator acknowledge the experience and position of the portfolio developer. For instance, the expectations for a principal's portfolio might be more complex than those for a first-year teacher, although the areas of evaluation could be the same.

Audience Assessment

In addition to the rubrics outlined in Figure 7.1, using the multimedia portfolio format requires that several other questions be asked. These questions relate to the ease of audience access to multimedia. They include the following:

- Who is the audience?
- What equipment do they have?
- Will they be overwhelmed or alienated if they receive a CD?
- Are the instructions for access clear?
- Can the material be downloaded quickly?

It is important to find the answers to these questions if the portfolio is to be relevant and effective for its intended audience. For example, while at a high-tech school or university a multimedia presentation on the Internet might be best, a simple disk or CD-ROM might be preferred at a

Rubrics for Portfolio Evaluation

	Excellent	*Satisfactory*	*Unsatisfactory*
Statement of purpose, philosophy, and values	Clearly describes purpose of the portfolio and the educational philosophy of the producer	Describes purpose of the portfolio and the educational philosophy of the producer	Not stated or unclear
Framework matching purpose, e.g., selection criteria, competency standards	Elements clearly identified and appropriate links made	Elements identified	The framework is not listed, does not match purpose, or is not clear
Suitable evidence for each criterion	Clear links made between evidence and element	Evidence available for each element	Evidence not related to the elements
Evidence consistent with underlying values	Links between evidence and underlying values are clearly expressed and demonstrated; shows the values in action	Evidence is congruent with the expressed educational philosophy and values	No link between evidence and underlying values
Evidence of a range of scales	Links made between evidence from classroom, schoolwide, and professional activities	Evidence chosen from classroom, schoolwide, and professional activities	Range not evident, e.g., relies on classroom evidence only
Evidence shows change over time, progress towards achievement of goals	Explicit evidence of progress towards goals, clearly articulated through reflection and synthesis	Time frame indicated, little stated evidence of growth	No time period or progress indicated
Various types of evidence to ensure reliability	Wide range of text, graphics, photographs, sound, video, etc., to meet the multiple intelligences; student work, feedback	More than one type of evidence, e.g., text plus photographs, or text plus video	Only one type of evidence
Appropriate amount of evidence	Reflection illuminates the evidence	Each piece of evidence provides new information	Too little evidence or repetition of evidence
Reflection on artifacts linking theory and practice	Clearly argued statement reflecting broad understanding of theory and practice	Statement identifying practices that reflect relevant educational theory	No theoretical underpinning expressed
Reflection on the overall portfolio	Statement links back to the philosophy of teaching and how the portfolio meets intended purpose	Reflective statement and brief review of intended purpose	No statement of overall reflection

FIGURE 7.1

school with less technological access. Some enthusiastic teachers have spent hours preparing multimedia portfolios on disk and sent them with job applications to particular schools only to find that no one looked at them!

At present, the greatest benefit in producing a multimedia portfolio is that teachers are able to gain technological skills while reflecting on their professional growth. Currently there is limited demand for job applications presented in multimedia format, but as technology develops, it won't be long before multimedia résumés or portfolios are preferred.

The checklist in Figure 7.2 provides portfolio developers with some guidelines to reference before publishing a multimedia portfolio. Some of the main aspects of development that can affect the communication of material are covered.

FIGURE 7.2

Developer Checklist for a Multimedia Portfolio

Checklist for a Multimedia Portfolio	*Yes*	*No*	*N/A*
Is there clarity of design?			
Is the text easy to read throughout the portfolio?			
Are the graphics quick to load?			
Are the graphics supported by text?			
Is navigation easy?			
Are the links obvious to the reader?			
Do the links lead to further information and lead back (no dead ends)?			
Is the use of color attractive?			
Is there a consistent style throughout?			
Are sound and video files clear and do they add to the information?			
Are sound and video labeled and supported by text?			
Are there contact details for the developer?			
Is copyright acknowledged appropriately?			
Is there a clear indication of production dates for the portfolio?			
If the portfolio has been updated, is there information related to this?			

Consulting this checklist can help you make sure your portfolio is set up properly and in an organized manner, which will enable the audience to access it easily.

It is important that all aspects of the personal evaluation described on page 84 be addressed before the portfolio is presented to an evaluator. This way, you are making sure you present your evaluator with the best possible portfolio product you can produce. Some important aspects of portfolios evaluators look for include:

- Awareness of the workplace and the position
- Using criteria which match the purpose of the portfolio (for example, the key selection criteria in a job application)
- Choosing evidence which reflects personal values and the chosen criteria

In addition, a digital portfolio shows an employer that you are innovative and aware of information technology and its uses.

Assessing Learning through Portfolio Development

A fundamental principle of this book is that educators will grow professionally as a result of producing a multimedia portfolio. They will learn more about using the Internet for research and for communicating with a global audience. They will become producers as well as consumers of multimedia technology, enabling them to become more confident about using multimedia in their daily work. This transfer of knowledge and skills will benefit not only themselves but their students, colleagues, and community. The following skills audit (Figure 7.3) is designed to track the development of basic multimedia skills. It should be used before beginning a multimedia portfolio project to identify current skills and professional development needs. After development is completed, the right-hand column can be used to record learning.

Completing this skills audit should allow you to see exactly what skills you have developed throughout the portfolio production process. Developing self-confidence about technological skills and becoming aware of the new skills you have cultivated will allow you to feel more comfortable when presenting your portfolio to an audience.

Multimedia Skills Audit

I feel confident that I have the following skills:

	Before production	*After production*
1. Finding Information on the Internet		
• research about portfolios	❑	❑
• research about teaching and learning	❑	❑
• research regarding class topics	❑	❑
2. Communicating via the Web		
• sending an e-mail message	❑	❑
• joining an e-mail group	❑	❑
• joining in online chat	❑	❑
3. Creating Multimedia		
• producing text pages in HTML	❑	❑
• scanning text and graphic material to digital form	❑	❑
• incorporating graphics in text pages	❑	❑
• creating sound and video files	❑	❑
• creating hypertext links between pages	❑	❑
• displaying material on a laptop computer	❑	❑
• writing material to CD-ROM	❑	❑
4. Publishing Information on the Internet		
• publishing files to server	❑	❑
• updating information	❑	❑
5. Using Multimedia in Curriculum and Administration		
• preparing classroom materials	❑	❑
• encouraging students to research on Internet	❑	❑
• encouraging students to use e-mail	❑	❑
• assisting students in developing multimedia	❑	❑
• recording school events and achievements	❑	❑

FIGURE 7.3

Public Presentation of Your Portfolio

Portfolios are designed for communication. To be effective, these points should be kept in mind:

- Equipment needs to be prepared and tested in advance of presentation time
- Audience should be able to see screen clearly
- Presenter needs to appear confident with the technology
- Presenter must maintain eye contact with the audience
- Multimedia material needs to support what the presenter says

Multimedia presentations can significantly increase the impact of a message. However, referring to a portfolio in an interview requires some preparation and rehearsal. The audience should be made aware of the existence of the portfolio in advance, so they are not surprised by this type of presentation. When using a laptop computer for presentation, make sure the portfolio presentation is set up in advance to avoid the delay of computer startup time. This can be done by turning on the computer and starting the program a few minutes prior to the interview. The computer should not be a distraction to the presenter or the panel, but rather a natural adjunct to the information verbally presented. It is helpful to rehearse a pathway through the multimedia presentation.

Some interviewers will want to make their own way through a multimedia portfolio, and this must be encouraged. It is important to make sure that all links work and can be engaged prior to the interview. Leaving a sample portfolio behind on disk or CD-ROM or providing a web address (URL) for the portfolio site can add a memorable element to the closing of an interview.

Once you have assessed your portfolio and have determined that it represents your skills, values, and vision, that it meets the needs for which it was developed, and that all the multimedia aspects are functional and clear, you are ready to share your portfolio with your intended audience. Chapter 8 discusses ways in which this can be done.

Chapter 8

Sharing the Learning: Global Networking

[In the future] teachers will have a facilitation role with students, as well as a trouble-shooting role with the technology and various software packages. They will have to put course material on-line and make sure it is maintained, and also monitor that any linkages they create are still operating. That's a tremendously different set of skills that you have to have.

—Wheeler 1996, p. 12

Educators have a responsibility to share their knowledge with colleagues and their students, and on a wider scale, with the global community. Working as a teacher or administrator in the Digital Age will require new skills and knowledge, but one individual cannot learn all the technological skills that exist. The traditional isolation of the teacher needs to change to a more collegial approach to learning and communicating. The resources of the whole world are available through communication technology, and by using this technology, educators can benefit from and contribute to the global knowledge sharing which is now possible.

As the role of the teacher changes rapidly and as technology influences education and society, developing a professional portfolio has become a beneficial way to augment learning about technology. In this technological age the opportunities for professional growth and learning are enormous and can be supported by portfolio development. Teachers have reported that portfolio development results in learning that is likely to fall into four main areas:

- learning about self and others
- learning about portfolio development
- learning about technology
- learning about teaching and learning

These four categories are explored in further detail below.

What Teachers Have Learned from Portfolio Development

Teachers who have been involved in multimedia portfolio development often notice that they have expanded their knowledge in the following areas:

- **Self-reflection.** Self-reflection is an important aspect of portfolio development for many teachers and often results in increased confidence. This leads some teachers to consider the role of others in their learning: colleagues, students, administrators, personal friends, and family. Teachers often realize that without input, insight, and encouragement from others, they would be less effective learners.
- **Portfolio development.** Many teachers are not initially familiar with the format of a portfolio, so through portfolio development they often gain information about the content, format, and audience of a portfolio. Teachers may learn more about their vision and values as they pertain to their profession when working on their Personal Statement. Teachers may also come to better understand their personal teaching style and in what areas they can improve upon by collecting information for their Personal Archive and reflecting on their work. In addition, while putting together their portfolio teachers may find that providing evidence of teaching effectiveness is easier than finding evidence of leadership and management skills. This results in teachers realizing the importance of keeping artifacts in a variety of forms—photographs, videos, and feedback from colleagues.
- **Technological skills.** When technology is used as a tool to achieve a particular purpose (as in multimedia portfolio development), teachers recognize that they have gained technological skills. Although teachers tend not to focus on these skills as much as on the influences and experiences contributing to their professional growth, the development of new techno-

logical skills is very important, as it can enable teachers to communicate with their students in new ways.

- **Expanding teaching skills.** Teachers who are learning about technology often encourage their students to learn with them. Once teachers become comfortable with technology, they can use it to develop new projects for their students, introduce students to new ways of gathering information, and encourage multisensory creativity and integrated communication projects among students. Additionally, teaching with technology is especially important to keep students current with the technology that is present everywhere in the Digital Age.

Educators who develop portfolios often report that the development process is as important as the product in encouraging reflective practice. Thus, feedback from colleagues can further assist teachers to meet technological challenges. Portfolio development can be undertaken alone, but it seems that greater learning occurs when groups of people work together. People who share in the process of portfolio development can act as critical supporters, mentors, and coaches for each other. In this way they can provide mutual feedback and support, inspiration, and encouragement. A skilled colleague can suggest resources, probe for explanation, critique a portfolio during its development, and celebrate its completion. By collaborating with others, teachers contribute to their own development, as well as to the development of the profession as a whole.

Collegial Learning Opportunities Provided by Portfolios

Working together, particularly on such a personal activity as a portfolio, is still a new idea for some teachers. However, setting aside time to work on portfolio development with a partner is certainly a means of encouraging professional dialogue. Some schools set aside time for this activity amongst mentor pairs, small teams, or even large numbers of staff. In some cases, networks between schools have been developed to encourage support for portfolio development while allowing for the sharing of ideas and development of joint school projects. This type of collaboration can be achieved through a variety of methods, the most common of which are detailed below.

Discussions and Presentations

It is very important that teachers discuss their work, and portfolio development provides a focus for such discussion. Teachers contribute to their own growth and to that of their colleagues when they present papers at workshops, conferences, and staff meetings. The general purpose of the portfolio is to communicate with others. Through the portfolio teachers can engage in a discourse about teaching and learning, self-discovery, or technical issues relating to their work.

Publishing

Publishing a portfolio is a very effective way of sharing information, as is publishing articles about the production process. Preparing a document for publication allows the writer to engage in a synthesis of ideas and thoughts. Publishing a document provides an opportunity for readers to respond to the ideas in the document, thereby creating a dialogue between readers and writers. Various professional networks, such as the National Network of Portfolio Users in the United States, publish newsletters to foster the sharing of ideas and discussion on the topic of portfolios.

Electronic Networks

Electronic networks, such as those described on the following page, can expand the collegial group, allowing for information exchange, feedback, and support. Simply sending a message to anyone can be the beginning of a network. The network can become a virtual learning community as ideas are tested, evidence shared, and feedback given. For such an online community to thrive, people need to be able to use communication technology. The simplest way for this to occur is through e-mail.

FIGURE 8.21

An E-Mail List for People Working on Portfolios

The following example will be done using the electronic network address for EL-PORT@UAA.ALASKA.EDU (an electronic network managed at the University of Alaska). When you are ready to send your own mail to the list, follow the directions below.

Sending Mail to the List

To send a message to all the people currently subscribed to the network list, just send mail to EL-PORT@UAA.ALASKA.EDU. This is called "sending mail to the list," because you send mail to a single address and MAILSERV makes copies for all the people who have subscribed. This address (EL-PORT@UAA.ALASKA.EDU) is also called the "list address."

Leaving the List (Unsubscribing)

You may leave the list at any time by sending a "UNSUBSCRIBE EL-PORT" command to MAILSERV@UAA.ALASKA.EDU.

(PMDF Mailserv V5.1,1998)

- List serves (e-mail)

A list serve provides individuals with an opportunity to join an electronic network with people who have like interests. List serves can be found on the World Wide Web by searching the words "list serve", which will bring up a large number of electronic lists on many topics. Usually the websites listed will have details about how to subscribe to one of these networks.

To subscribe to an e-mail list serve, you must have access to the following:

1. a computer with modem,
2. a connection to an Internet Service Provider (ISP),
3. the use of an e-mail address to send and receive mail.

The example above (Figure 8.1) shows how to send mail to an e-mail list where people all around the world who are interested in portfolios can post messages and ask questions.

Another portfolio network is the cutting edge list based in Melbourne, Australia. To subscribe, send an e-mail message to majordomo@mars.eu.rmit.edu.au, and in the body of the message write "subscribe cutting edge" followed by your e-mail address.

Different lists will provide different instructions for subscribing and leaving that list.

Online Chat and Discussion Groups

Various discussion groups (both synchronous and asynchronous) exist on the Internet. Many people are joining such groups based on particular topics or areas of interest. Keep in mind that these discussion groups are in a global forum, where timeframes, experiences, and customs are different for everyone. In other words, don't assume that everyone's experiences will be the same as yours. Some chats take place in real time and are often organized in advance. In this case, a calendar of chat topics will be available. To find a chat or discussion group, you can search the Internet using "chat" or "education chat" as keywords.

E-mail transcends time zone constraints and the costs of communicating to faraway places via phone, making it a good vehicle for discussions and the sharing of ideas. Partaking in a chat or discussion group can also introduce teachers to the teaching and learning experiences of people all over the world.

Websites about Portfolios

Websites provide another means of publishing information and sharing ideas. The following websites have been established to share information about portfolios and may be useful for gathering new ideas on portfolio development.

http://transition.alaska.edu/www/portfolios.html

This site is managed by Helen Barrett at the University of Alaska Anchorage School of Education. It focuses on hardware and software for electronic portfolios for students and teachers.

http://www.pedanet.jyu.fi/cato/study1.html

Marja Kankaanranta at the Institute for Educational Research University of Jyväskylä (Finland) has conducted research on digital portfolios. Her website includes information on this research, including a project on kindergarten teachers who are assessing their professional growth and learning through the use of portfolios presented on the web.

http://www.nwrel.org/

The North West Regional Educational Laboratory website provides an annotated bibliography of resources related to portfolio development. The books, articles, and electronic resources listed provide suggestions and guidelines for preparing, producing, and evaluating portfolios.

http://amby.com/kimeldorf/sampler/

Martin Kimeldorf, author and former teacher, has a multimedia portfolio sampler on his website. This site provides ideas and information for people who wish to develop their own portfolios.

http://www.tc.cc.va.us/faculty/tcreisd/resource/webfolio/intro.htm

At Tidewater Community College in Virginia, Donna Reiss provides online instructions to her students to assist them in portfolio development. This is an open site for all to read.

http://www.teachnet.com/how-to/employment/portfolios/index.html

This is a commercial site that gives information on resources that can be used to market portfolio development.

http://www.cuttingedge.rmit.edu.au

This site focuses on multimedia portfolio development.

Interacting with the online learning community provides teachers with a global perspective, as people from many countries can communicate without ever meeting each other in person. Electronic networking can also provide opportunities for teachers to work together globally on projects, to get feedback on professional development activities, or even to plan international exchange visits. Putting a finished portfolio on the web can also open the door for a dialogue with the global community.

As more and more teachers design projects and courses for an on-line community of learners, they will see that the skills of multimedia production and electronic networking are fundamental for global information sharing. In this Digital Age, courses from schools, colleges, and universities in the U.S. and Australia can be taken by someone with a computer in Indonesia or the U.K. Multimedia portfolio development can act as a useful introduction to this new world of learning. Chapter 9 discusses how educators and administrators can successfully integrate this type of learning into their schools.

Chapter 9

Professional Growth through Portfolio Development

"Reflecting on accomplishments reminds people they are really making a meaningful contribution—something all too easy to forget when they are drowning in relentless demands. People also understand that if the "worst" happens, and they lose their job, they have skills that can be used on other work."

—Moses 1997, p. 207

Portfolios have been used for student assessment for many years and are becoming more common as tools for both the professional growth and assessment of teachers. In the twenty-first century, evidence of achievements and outcomes is necessary to market oneself, making a portfolio an asset for every student, teacher, and administrator. Schools and organizations that wish to give their students and teachers every opportunity to grow can implement portfolio development. The benefits of such a project will be reaped through improved teaching and learning and enhanced self-esteem. Portfolios allow the whole organization to celebrate its capability and achievements.

When conducting research for this book, we found many administrators, school leaders, and classroom teachers who would like to be more involved in "a portfolio approach" to developing a learning organization. They expressed great interest in the possibility of linking professional development in technology with the creation of portfolios.

However, few have implemented portfolio programs in their organization. This is often due to a lack of understanding of the nature of portfolios and their purposes, enormous demands which leave teachers and administrators little time to plan and reflect, and limited knowledge about the possibilities of technology. However, these issues can be addressed to enact a portfolio approach in any organization.

Implementing a Portfolio Approach

Many school administrators have refrained from developing a portfolio approach within their organization because they are unaware of what a portfolio can accomplish and they don't know how or where to begin. However, implementing a portfolio approach doesn't have to be so difficult.

The many benefits of a portfolio have been discussed throughout this book. It serves as a vehicle of self-reflection, allowing the teachers to examine themselves and their successes in order to evaluate their abilities. Such self-reflection results in improved teaching and learning as teachers develop self-confidence about their skills and learn new ways of communicating with others. The portfolio can also serve as a representative of the whole school community—a compilation of the strengths and accomplishments of the entire staff. In this way the portfolio can be used as a marketing tool for the entire school. The development process of the portfolio is also a benefit in and of itself, because it advances the developer's technological skills. Teachers can then pass on what they learned to their students. This type of sharing of knowledge is a very important facet of portfolio development. Knowledge that is developed through the portfolio process can be shared with other students and teachers in order to further their development as well.

Although administrators may be aware of the benefits of portfolio development, they may be intimidated by the idea of implementing such an approach in their organization. However, it is not a difficult process. First, staff needs to be made aware of the many benefits portfolios can provide. This will provide them with an understanding of what it is they are creating and how they can benefit from portfolio production. As mentioned in Chapter 8, there are many examples of portfolios on the World Wide Web that can be easily accessed. These can serve as models, structured formats, guidelines, and examples of different types of portfolios. These need to be provided in order to familiarize staff with the basic structure of portfolios. Once this is done, training and technical support should be available, preferably in a school-based setting, with a focus on processes such as planning, development, reflection, and self-evaluation. Courses in portfolio development are offered by various universities and training organizations and can be given to whole school communities upon request. These courses often include self-awareness and planning tools, guidelines for portfolio structures, and ways to evaluate portfolios. Additionally, the portfolio approach is more likely to be successful when time for production and reflection is incorporated into teachers' work expectations. Some schools require teachers to present a portfolio on an annual basis, and they allow time each week for teachers to meet to work together on their portfolios. In this way the portfolio is integrated into the teacher's working life.

It is important to remember that a portfolio approach to professional growth is an innovation and therefore needs to be given time and support for successful implementation. Green and Smyser (1996) suggest that a planning timeline of at least three years should be allowed for complete implementation of a portfolio approach in a school, beginning with a pilot project which includes teacher training and partnering for work on development of the portfolios. The teachers in the pilot project then become mentors to the next group. As with any innovation, it is wise to take time to spread the process throughout the school. Begin with those teachers who are ready to try something new, and encourage them to share their experiences and knowledge with other teachers. During this process, the focus is on the meaning of good teaching, aspects of such teaching, and verifiable evidence of this. This type of focus can be achieved through discussion, through consideration of values and vision through portfolio development, and through self-reflection and feedback from others.

The individual and the community benefit most from the portfolio development process when there are opportunities for collaboration during production, for presentation to audiences, and to receive feedback. For example, in one school, teachers are invited to prepare portfolios for performance review, but it is not a requirement. Once each term, a week is planned to focus on professional development, share success stories, and engage in development planning. Students are also required to prepare portfolios that focus on their growth through learning. The school principal models learning to the staff and students by keeping a learning journal and maintaining a professional portfolio. Teachers in performance assessment teams are encouraged to discuss and share their portfolios. In this school, the "portfolio approach" has been developed over several years as a natural behavior of a learning community.

Engaged Learning through Technology

The Digital Age requires a vision of a learning community where all learners are engaged, where teachers are learners and learners are teachers. School communities that have already developed such a vision are well-prepared for this new era. According to Jones, Valdez, Nowakoski, and Rasmussen (1995) engaged learning can be promoted through technology. Thus, when technology can be used for a purpose that is "real" to the learner, the learning is able to meeet the needs of learners with different learning styles. This provides learners with an opportunity to learn with and through the technology. In this way, technology can be used to help different learners meet their learning goals and needs.

Indicators of high technology performance are shown in Figure 9.1. These indicators demonstrate what the school of the twenty-first century might be like and how technology can be used to support learning goals. These indicators provide administrators and teachers with a framework for decision-making related to the use of technology for engaged learning.

Indicators of High Technology Performance

Variable	*Indicator of High Technology Performance*	*Indicator Definition*
Access	Connective	Schools are connected to the Internet and other resources
	Ubiquitous	Technology resources and equipment are persuasive and conveniently located for individual (as opposed to centralized) use
	Interconnective	Students and teachers interact by communicating and collaborating in diverse ways
	Designed for equitable use	All students have access to rich, challenging learning opportunities and interactive, generative instruction
Operability	Interoperable	Capable of exchanging data easily among diverse formats and technologies
	Open architecture	Allows users to access third-party hardware/software
	Transparent	Users are not—and do not need to be—aware of how the hardware/software operates

FIGURE 9.1

(continued on next page)

Indicators of High Technology Performance

Variable	*Indicator of High Technology Performance*	*Indicator Definition*
Organization	Distributed	Technology/system resources are not centralized, but exist across any number of people, environments, and situations
	Designed for user contributions	Users can provide input/resources to the technology/system on demand
	Designed for collaborative projects	Technology is designed to facilitate communication among users with diverse systems/equipment
Engageability	Access to challenging tasks	Technology offers or allows access to tasks, data, and learning opportunities that stimulate thought and inquiry
	Enables learning by doing	Technology offers access to simulations, goals-based learning, and real-world problems
	Provides guided participation	Technology responds intelligently to user and is able to diagnose and prescribe new learning
Ease of Use	Effective help	Technology provides help indices that are more than glossaries; may provide procedures for tasks and routines
	User-friendliness/user control	Technology facilitates user and is free from overly complex procedures; user can easily access data and tools on demand
	Fast	Technology has a fast processing speed and is not "down" for long periods of time
	Available training and support	Training is readily and conveniently available, as is ongoing support
	Provides just enough information just in time	Technology allows for random access, multiple points of entry, and different levels and types of information
Functionality	Diverse tools	Technology enables access to full diversity of generic and context-specific tools basic to learning and working in the 21st century
	Media use	Technology provides opportunity to use media technologies
	Promotes programming and authoring	Technology provides tools (e.g., "wizards") that are used to make other tools
	Supports project design skills	Technology facilitates the development of skills related to project design and implementation

FIGURE 9.1 (continued)

Many of the indicators in Figure 9.1 are supported by undertaking the developmental processes necessary for using multimedia to produce portfolios, and they also can be applied to a range of other activities for teachers and students. Technology must be accessible, challenging, and useful if learners are to become active producers. With clear goals, focusing first on the learning and then on the technology, it is less likely that vast sums of money will be spent on technology that does not support the learning. It is important that goals are developed first, and then computer technology and programs can be found that meets those goals. Augmenting teacher and student learning with technology can empower both teachers and students by placing the control in their hands. The possibilities are endless when teachers and students work together on portfolio projects to foster their learning and development through technology.

Using a Portfolio for Marketing Purposes

Portfolios can be used for many purposes, and one of the main ways portfolios can be used is for marketing oneself or an organization. The multimedia portfolio may be the marketing tool of the future. It is more complete than the standard résumé or application form because it provides a wider range of evidence of achievements through visual and audio formats as well as text, and it allows the reader to explore the layers of information without being overwhelmed by large amounts of material. It also provides tangible evidence of experience or achievements.

In order to create a portfolio that will effectively market oneself or one's organization, it is important to have a deep understanding of oneself. In her book *Career Intelligence,* Barbara Moses (1997) suggests that the following four principles are important for individuals managing their career:

- be a career activist: craft your own future;
- know yourself: know who you are, what you are good at, the contents of your personal portfolio, what you have to sell. Redefine your experiences to identify underlying themes and skills;
- know what you love: know what is most important to you;
- be who you are: see yourself as capable; develop a personal success paradigm (pp. 138–139).

Many teachers will benefit from spending time reflecting on themselves and applying these principles. The portfolio inherently supports these principles, and thus, teachers who develop portfolios are in a better position to craft their own future. The vast range of self-help books regarding career advancement has now been supplemented by websites offering assistance to those who are looking for a new job, wanting to advance their career, or wanting to distinguish themselves from the competition. These sources can be used to augment the portfolio as a marketing tool.

Linking Individual Ambitions with Organizational Objectives

The learning organization is made up of many individual learners moving forward to achieve personal and organizational goals. The portfolio approach has the capacity to support organizational objectives through its structure, whether the purpose is for professional development planning, performance review, or employment application. The elements which form the framework for the portfolio can be based on or include reference to the organization's strategic goals. Where evaluation rubrics require reference to strategic goals, individuals must reflect on their contribution to these goals. When information is recorded in a portfolio, organizations are able to ascertain whether individuals are aligning with strategic goals and thus are able to achieve a clearer sense of staff capabilities and achievements.

At one elementary school, some of the main goals of the school center around furthering technological growth. The principal suggests that teachers have the power to achieve school objectives regarding such growth.

> "Innovative teachers challenge every teacher to help build 21st Century schools by committing to 3 actions:
> - build their own expertise in using new learning technologies
> - share expertise with students as part of their daily process
> - work to make classroom technology available to all students and teachers" (Guilieri 1998).

These three actions can be clearly linked as teachers, administrators, and students engage in learning through a multimedia portfolio approach. The portfolio is an exciting opportunity for professional development and to promote learning goals and further technology usage in organizations at the cutting edge of teaching and learning. The multimedia portfolio is a multifaceted tool which can be used to fill several different purposes, but the most important purpose it has is that it promotes learning among both students and teachers. This type of portfolio will be an important asset to schools and individuals as society heads into the Digital Age.

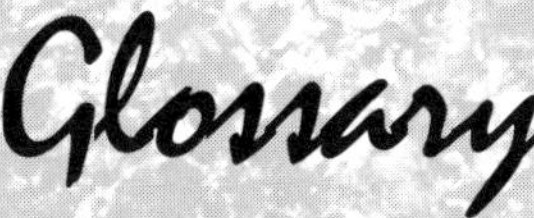

Glossary

animation. The technique of making something "come alive" through the use of movements or actions.

artifact. A specific piece of evidence contained in the Personal Archive. These pieces are linked together to develop a professional portfolio.

browser. Computer software that allows computers to read HTML documents and graphics and also allows for Internet access. Some common browsers are Netscape Gold™, Mosaic™, Netscape Navigator™, and Microsoft Internet Explorer™.

baud rate. The speed of a modem. Faster modems are preferable because they reduce the amount of time it takes to connect e-mail and Internet users online, resulting in lower user costs.

bookmark. This is also called "favorites" and allows the URL of favorite sites to be saved so it can be clicked upon for easy return in the future.

CD-ROM (Compact disk or CD). Compact Disk-Read Only Memory disks are disks similar to music CDs. They allow the user to store large amounts of digitized data and thus are a useful way to store a multimedia portfolio.

chat (online). Conversation that is carried out by writing messages back and forth in real time over the Internet.

data base. A storage system used for large amounts of information that is organized into categories to make retrieval of the information easier.

digitized (digital) data. Information that has been saved in digitized form from audio and video recordings, graphics, and still and moving images.

e-mail. Electronic mail is an Internet service through which the user can send and receive messages.

FTP. File Transfer Protocol is a method of transferring files to and from an Internet server.

GIF. Graphic Interchange Format is the term used for compressed files that are in indexed color mode (8 bit color). All graphical web browsers support this format.

home page. The first page in a website or the introductory door to the site.

http. Hyper Text Transfer Protocol is a method of transferring hypertext documents. It is an indicator of which protocol (preferred method of operating) to use.

hypertext. Hypertext refers to a document that contains links to other documents. Hypertext is engaged when the computer allows the user to link various pieces of text or information to various other pieces of text or information.

Internet. This is a worldwide information network provided by telecommunications companies. The Internet is accessible through the computer via a modem. The Internet allows for global exchange of information.

ISP. The Internet Service Provider is a company or agency that sells accounts which allow people to dial into the Internet.

JPG/JPEG. In Joint Photographic Experts Group files, files are compressed into smaller files while color images and tones remain optimized.

laptop. This is a small but relatively powerful computer that weighs no more than a textbook. It can be powered by a battery or by a traditional AC/DC power supply. It is very portable and can fit inside a briefcase easily.

list serve. A way that subscribers to an e-mail address (list serve) can send and receive messages to communicate with all other subscribers.

modem. A small unit connecting the computer with telephone lines. The modem electronically converts computer-generated information which is then relayed backwards and forwards across the telephone lines and into its original screen format.

multimedia. Multimedia is a general term that covers the combination of text, graphics, sound, and video in digital form.

multimedia (digital) portfolio. A collection of evidence of achievements presented through various electronic formats, such as graphics, video, audio, or textual links.

PDF. Portable Document Format allows documents such as magazines to be read in original formats saved for reading via a computer file. This is not the same as HTML, and such files are often read using Adobe Acrobat™.

plug-ins. Files which allow multimedia components, such as audio and video, to be accessed via the Internet.

search engine. A sophisticated Internet tool that compiles indexes of information found on the Internet using keywords or phrases. The search engine provides the user with a list of matches for the keyword.

scanner. A scanner is about the size of a small printer. It can scan a page of text, a still photograph, or a diagram into a computer. The scanned document can then be included on screen in a multimedia presentation or in a printed publication.

server. A computer using server software which allows information to be stored and sent to Internet users.

synchronous and asynchronous communication. In synchronous communication interaction is direct, such as with a telephone conversation or networking in "real-time". In asynchronous communication there is a time difference between sending the message and receiving the reply, such as is the case with facsimiles or e-mail.

URL. Uniform Resource Locator is the World Wide Web address for a document. The URL is made up of the following sequence of information: protocol, host name, path, filename: http://rmit, edu.au, indexhtml

video conferencing. Video conferencing requires participants to be linked by two-way video and audio. A common configuration for such conferencing is to have both groups set up around a table within range of video cameras.

World Wide Web. A network of sites on the Internet that provide information and services to Internet users.

Bibliography

Armitage, C. (1998). The benefits of a pause for thought. *The Australian* [newspaper], December 16, 1998, 16.

Ashley, R. and Etherington, I. (1995). *Portfolios and presenting evidence of achievement.* U.K.: Pearson Publishing.

Association for Supervision and Curriculum Development (ASCD). (1996). Teacher portfolios: tools for improving teaching and learning. *Education Update 38,* December, 1-6.

Baron, C. (1996). *Creating your digital portfolio: A guide to marketing and self-promotion.* Indianapolis, IN: Hayden Books.

Barrett, H. (1997). *Collaborative planning for electronic portfolios: Asking strategic questions.* In the proceedings of the National Educational Computing Conference, Seattle, Washington.

Bridges, W. (1995). *Jobshift: How to prosper in a workplace without jobs.* London: Nicholas Brealey.

Brown, G., and Irby, B. (1995). The Portfolio: Should it also be used by administrators? *NASSP Bulletin,* April, 82–85.

Brown, G., and Irby, B. (1997). *The principal portfolio.* Thousand Oaks, CA: Corwin Press.

Burke, K., Fogarty, R., and Belgrad, S. (1994). *The mindful school: The portfolio connection.* Melbourne: Hawker Brownlow Education.

Burke, K. (Ed.) (1996a). *Professional portfolios: A collection of articles.* Melbourne: Hawker Brownlow Education.

Burke, K. (1996b). *Designing professional portfolios for change.* Melbourne: Hawker Brownlow Education.

Campbell, D., Cignetti, P., Melenyzer, B., Nettles, D., and Wyman, R. (1997). *How to develop a professional portfolio: A manual for teachers.* New York: Allyn and Bacon.

Case, S. H. (1994). Will mandating portfolios undermine their value? *Educational Leadership,* October, 46–47.

Cerbin, W. (1995). Connecting assessment of learning to improvement of teaching through the course portfolio. *Assessment Update No. 7,* January-February, 4–6.

Covey, S. (1992). *Principle-centered leadership.* New York: Simon and Schuster.

Culham, R. E. (1996). *Alternative assessment: Portfolios from the inside out.* Portland, OR: Northwest Regional Educational Laboratory.

Department of Education and Training (NSW). (1998). *School leadership strategy.* Sydney: Training and Development Directorate.

Diez, M. (1996). The portfolio: Sonnet, mirror and map. In Burke, K. (Ed). *Professional portfolios: A collection of articles.* Melbourne: Hawker Brownlow Education.

Dietz, M. (1998). *Journals as frameworks for change.* Arlington Heights, IL: Skylight Professional Development.

Dietz, M. (1998). *Portfolio Newsletter. Vol. 9,* Fall. Oxford, OH: NSDC.

Fullan, M. (1995). *Change forces.* Bristol, PA: The Falmer Press.

Gardner, H. (1984). *Frames of mind: The theory of multiple intelligences.* London: Heinemann.

Green, J. and Smyser, S. (1996). *The teacher portfolio: A strategy for professional development and evaluation.* Lancaster, PA: Technomic.

Handy, C. (1990). *The age of unreason.* Cambridge, MA: Harvard Business School Press.

Handy, C. (1994). *The empty raincoat: Making sense of the future.* London: Arrow Business.

Hargreaves, A. and Fullan, M. (Eds.) (1996). *Understanding teacher development.* New York: Cassell.

Harrison, R. (1984). Leadership and strategy for new age. In Adams, J. (Ed.) *Transforming work: A collection of organizational transformation readings.* Alexandria, VA: Miles River Press.

Hartnell-Young, E. (1998). Teachers as learners: Using portfolios for continuing development. In Beale, M. (Ed.) *Leading professional development: Beyond the classroom.* Melbourne: Hawker Brownlow Education.

Hartnell-Young, E. and Morriss, M. (1998). *Professional portfolios at the cutting edge.* Melbourne: RMIT [Royal Melbourne Institute of Technology] University.

Honey, P., and Mumford, A. (1986). *The manual of learning styles.* Maidenhead, Berkshire: Peter Honey.

Jones, M. and Martin, J. (1994). *Replay recognition of prior learning program.* Melbourne: Swinburne University of Technology.

Kimeldorf, M. (1995). *Creating portfolios for success in school, work, and life.* (Edited by P. Espeland). Melbourne: Hawker Brownlow Australia.

Kimeldorf, M. (1997). *Portfolio power: The new way to showcase all your job skills and experience.* Princeton, NJ: Peterson's Publishing Group.

Lemay, L. (1995). *Teach yourself web publishing with HTML in a week.* Indianapolis, IN: Sam's Publishing.

Martin-Kniep, G. (1996). *Teachers as learners in the portfolio design process.* Sea Cliff, NY: Learner-Centered Initiatives Ltd.

McLaughlin, M. and Vogt, M. (1996). *Portfolios in teacher education.* Newark, Delaware: International Reading Association.

McLaughlin, M. and Vogt, M. (1998). *Professional portfolio models: Reflections across the teaching profession.* Norwood, MA: Christopher-Gordon Publishers.

McLean, C. (1998). Unpublished portfolio.

Moses, B. (1997) *Career intelligence: The twelve new rules for work and life success.* San Francisco, CA: Berrett-Koehler Publishers Inc.

National Council for the Accreditation of Teacher Education (USA). (1995). *Curriculum guidelines for advanced programs in educational leadership for principals, superintendents, curriculum directors and supervisors.* Alexandria, VA: The Educational Leadership Constituent Council.

Paris, S. and Ayres, L. R. (1994). *Becoming reflective students and teachers with portfolios and authentic assessment.* Washington, D.C.: American Psychological Association.

Raymond, D., Butt, R. and Townsend, D. (1996). Contexts for teacher development. In Hargreaves, A. and Fullan, M. (Eds.) *Understanding teacher development.* New York: Cassell.

Rényi, J. (1996). *Teachers take charge of their learning: Transforming professional development for student success.* Washington, DC: National Foundation for the Improvement of Education.

Rifkin, J. (1994). *The end of work: The decline of the global labor force and the dawn of the post-market era.* New York: Putnam.

Schon, D. (1987). *Educating the reflective practitioner.* San Francisco, CA: Jossey-Bass.

Seldin, P. (1993). *Successful use of teaching portfolios.* Bolton, MA: Anker Publishing.

Seldin, P. (1997). *The teaching portfolio.* Bolton, MA: Anker Publishing.

Senge, P. (1994). *The fifth discipline: The art and practice of the learning organization.* Sydney: Random House.

Spender, D. (1995). *Nattering on the net.* Melbourne: Spinifex.

Standards Council of the Teaching Profession (Victoria). (1997). *Preparing a professional portfolio.* Melbourne: Standards Council of the Teaching Profession (Victoria).

University of Bradford U.K. (1998). *Personal development portfolio.* Unpublished guidelines.

University of Western Australia, Centre for Staff Development. (1998). *A guide to teaching portfolios and their role in promotion and tenure.* Nedlands, WA: The University of Western Australia.

Wheeler, L. (1996). Getting down to business. In *The webs we weave: Experiences in online teaching and learning at RMIT.* Melbourne: Flexible Learning Environment Unit, RMIT University.

Wheeler, L. (1997). *Online networks in VET research report.* Brisbane: Australian National Training Authority (ANTA).

Wiedmer, Terry. (1998). Digital Portfolios: Capturing and Demonstrating Skills and Levels of Performance. *Phi Delta Kappan* April, 586–589.

Wilcox, B. (1996). Smart portfolios for teachers in training. *The Journal of Adolescent and Adult Literacy 40,* November, 172-179.

Winograd, P. and Jones, D. L. (1993). The use of portfolios in performance assessment. *Portfolio News 4,* 1-13.

Winsor, P. (1997). *A guide to the development of professional portfolios in the faculty of education.* Lethbridge, Alberta: University of Lethbridge.

Wolf, K. (1994). Teaching portfolios: Capturing the complexity of teaching. In Ingvarson, L. and Chadbourne, R. (Eds). *New directions in teacher appraisal.* Melbourne: ACER.

Wolf, K., Whinery, B., and Hagerty, P. (1995). Teaching portfolios and portfolio conversations for teacher educators, teachers, and students. *Action in Teacher Education 17,* Spring, 30-39.

Wolf, K. (1996a). Developing an effective teaching portfolio. In Burke, K. (Ed). *Professional portfolios: A collection of articles.* Melbourne: Hawker Brownlow Education.

Wolf, K. (1996b). The schoolteacher's portfolio: Issues in design, implementation and evaluation. In Burke, K. (Ed). *Professional portfolios: A collection of articles.* Melbourne: Hawker Brownlow Education.

Wolf, K. and Siu-Runyan, Y. (1996). Portfolio purposes and possibilities. *Journal of Adolescent and Adult Literacy 40,* September, 30-37.

World Wide Web Documents

Bail, K. (1998). *Log on or drop out: Women in a wired world.* The 1998 Pamela Denoon Lecture. Retrieved April 23, 1999 from the World Wide Web: http://www.tip.net.au/other/wel/announce/denoon/98.pdl.htm.

Barrett, H. (1998). *Strategic questions.* Learning & Leading with technology, October. Retrieved April 23, 1999 from http://transition.alaska. edu/www/portfolios/LLTOct98.html.

Baume, D. (1997). *"We want to use portfolios to judge whether teachers should receive both an academic qualification and a professional qualification or accreditation."* Retrieved April 13, 1998 from the World Wide Web: http://www.lgu.ac.uk/deliberations/portfolios/baume1.html.

Boulware, B., Holt, Johnson, and Bratina, T. (1997). *Developing professional teaching portfolios using CD-ROM technology as a teaching-learning tool.* Paper presented at the Society for Information Technology and Teacher Education. 8th International Conference, April 14, 1997, Orlando, FL. Retrieved May 8, 1998 from the World Wide Web http://www.unf. edu/~tbratina/cdrom.htm.

Center for Teaching Excellence, Iowa State University. (1997). *How to document your teaching.* Retrieved April 23, 1999 from the World Wide Web: http://teach.admin.iastate.edu/CTE/port.html.

Chang, P. (1997). *Suggested contents of a teaching portfolio.* Retrieved April 23, 1999 from the World Wide Web: http://www.unc.edu/~edci/portfoli.htm.

Cook, D. and Kessler, J. (1994). *The professional teaching portfolio.* Retrieved April 23, 1999 from the World Wide Web: http://www. mnsfld.edu/~mlambert/prosem/portfolio.html.

Delaney, B. and Dyson, C. (1998). *Women: Creating the connection.* Melbourne: Office of Training and Further Education. Retrieved April 23, 1999 from the World Wide Web: www.otfe.vic.gov.au/mmedia/women.

Doolittle, P. (1994). *Teacher portfolio assessment.* ERIC Clearinghouse on Assessment and Evaluation, Washington, D.C. ED385608 . Retrieved May 5, 1998 from the World Wide Web: http://www.spectra.net/~cfthree/portfolio/DOCS/portfolio2.html.

Edith Cowan University. (1998). *Guidelines for writing a teaching portfolio.* Retrieved April 23, 1999 from the World Wide Web: http://www.cowan.edu.au/eddev/tchport/tchcont.htm.

Griffith University. (1998). *Teaching portfolios: Guidelines for academic staff.* Retrieved April 23, 1999 from the World Wide Web: http://www.gu.edu.au/gwis/gihe/tp_guidecont.html.

Guilieri, M. (1998). *Rationale for change and a new vision for education in the 21st century.* Retrieved August 22, 1998 from the World Wide Web: http://www.enps.vic.edu.au/tchlearn/rationale.html.

Johnson, J. Kaplan, J., and Marsh, S. (1996). *Professional teaching portfolios: A catalyst for rethinking education.* Retrieved March 28, 1998 from the World Wide Web: http://educ.queensu.ca/projects/action_research/jjohnson.htm.

Jones, B., Valdez, G., Nowakoski, J., and Rasmussen, C. (1995). *Designing Learning and Technology for educational reform.* Washington, DC: North Central Regional Education Laboratory. Retrieved April 23, 1999 from the World Wide Web: http://www.ncrel.org/sdrs/edtalk/newtimes.htm

Kimeldorf, M. (1997). *Portfolio sampler.* Retrieved April 23, 1999 from the World Wide Web: http://amby.com/kimeldorf/

Mandia, K. (1998) *Kelly's portfolio on the web.* Retrieved April 23, 1999 from the World Wide Web: http://www.mandia.com/kelly/portfolio. htm.

Niguidula, D. (1993). *The digital portfolio: A richer picture of student performance.* Retrieved April 23, 1999 from the World Wide Web: http://www.essential schools.org/pubs/exhib_schdes/dp/html

Reiss, D. (1998). Retrieved April 23, 1999 from the World Wide Web: http://www.tc.cc.va. us/faculty/tcreisd/resource/webfolio/intro.htm

Riggs, I. and Sandlin, R. (1998). *Utilizing teacher portfolios to support and assess new teachers.* Retrieved July 26, 1998 from the World Wide Web: http://www.auburn.edu/academic/education/tpi/riggs.html.

Taylor, C. (1997). Unpublished multimedia portfolio.

Women@the cutting edge.(1997). *Developing your professional portfolio.* Available: http://www.cuttingedge.rmit.edu.au.

Index